Who knew learning new vocabularıch fun. I homeschool my two teens. The   ı a couple of days. When they finished,   can't wait for the next volume." — **Cindy Fuller**, mother, homeschooler

"Although *Visualize Your Vocabulary* is primarily for high school students studying for the SAT, it's not just for students. I wanted my son to read it, but he had to wait for me to finish it, which didn't take long. It is so entertaining I could hardly put it down." — **Lindsey Masterson**, parent, avid reader

"I have always been more analytical and mathematically gifted. As a typical boy, I whizzed through math in school and I loved taking things apart to see how they worked. However, when it came to reading and memorizing, I felt like I was being punished. If only I could have learned vocabulary the *Visualize Your Vocabulary* way." — **Ryan Aslan**, Sensei, Personal Trainer Instructor, NASM, A-CPT, NPTI

"*Visualize Your Vocabulary* teaches an imaginative way to learn new words. Skipping the trite advice and insipid lists in order to bring a colorful new strategy to bear, the author gives fascinating information and creative mnemonics that will help anyone looking to expand their vocabulary in everyday life." — **Desirae Westberg**, avid reader

Visualize Your Vocabulary

**Turn Any SAT Word into a Picture
and Remember It Forever**

Shayne Gardner

To my daughter Savannah, who keeps the eye rolling and sighing to a minimum every time I ask, "Do you know what that word means?" or "Do you know what that means in Latin?"

"…of making many books there is no end, and much study is weariness of the flesh." —Ecclesiastes 12:12

Visualize Your Vocabulary: Turn Any SAT Word into a Picture and Remember It Forever

By Shayne Gardner

Illustrations: Kris Hagen

Editing: Ann N. Videan

A portion of the proceeds from Visualize Your Vocabulary goes to:

Lost Dog & Cat Rescue Foundation

Mercury One

Marine Corps – Law Enforcement Foundation

Library of Congress Catalog Card Number: 2014909151

ISBN-13: 978-1499500448

ISBN-10: 1499500440

Printed by CreateSpace

VisualizeYourVocabulary.com

Facebook.com/VisualizeYourVocabulary

VisualizeYourVocabulary@gmail.com

Table of Contents

Introduction

Why this book?

If you read *Visualize Your Vocabulary* and use this mnemonic aid for other SAT words not included here, you will gain a remarkable edge over students who do not. You will ingest the academic equivalent of steroids for an athlete.

The reason for this book is simple. We think in pictures. Studies show most people are visual learners. The brain remembers pictures better than words. So if you want to learn new words as fast as possible, and actually enjoy it, simply turn your words into pictures and skip the rote memorization.

Who should read this book?

Anyone who wants to expand their vocabulary should study this book. However, all 250 of the vocabulary words in *Visualize Your Vocabulary* are SAT words. So it is essential for anyone studying for the SAT, ACT, or any other standardized college entrance exams. It is also excellent for learning-disabled students, whether they are college bound or not.

How it works

The simple trick of turning a word into a picture is called a mnemonic. We have used these memory techniques from early childhood without much awareness of it. For instance, we learned our ABCs to the tune of the nursery rhyme *Twinkle, Twinkle, Little Star.* Mnemonics can be used to learn anything from algebraic formulas and history to grammar rules.

My favorite memory technique is converting the abstract definition of a word into a concrete "thing" I can visualize in my mind's eye. Many times a difficult word I want to memorize doesn't want to stick without a mnemonic. However, if I take the time to turn it into a picture, it sticks like super glue and I never forget it.

What you have to do is come up with something already familiar that rhymes with the word you want to learn. This rhyme word serves as the link or bridge connecting the word to the picture definition. I call this link word the memory word. Next, you turn the definition into a picture that includes the memory word. As an example, take the word "alacrity." It is a noun meaning "cheerful eagerness or readiness to respond; liveliness." My memory word is "a black kitty," because it is a near perfect rhyme. My picture for alacrity is:

> Your **black kitty** is quite unusual. You return home after a long day at school and your six-foot-tall black kitty, who can walk on his hind legs, **cheerfully and eagerly** runs out to greet you. He does a few somersaults, grabs your backpack with a smile on his face, and carries it for you. Once inside, he pulls off your shoes, puts your slippers on your feet, cartwheels into the kitchen to pour your favorite drink, and lies down at your feet purring.

It's that simple. I used the rhyme word as a substitute to link to the action picture describing the word. Now when I hear or see the word "alacrity," I simply think of what it sounds like and the picture definition comes flooding into my mind.

Rules of the game

A few simple rules make the picture stick like glue. If you don't use these rules when creating your own picture, you will certainly find it too boring and bland. Boring won't work and you will forget it.

Rule #1   Make the picture impossible, crazy, and illogical. In my picture for alacrity, the kitty is six feet tall, walks on its hind legs, carries a backpack, and does somersaults and cartwheels. Not possible. If the picture is too logical or is possible, you will not remember it. Crazy jumps out at you and is easily remembered.

Rule #2   Action! This is often incorporated in with Rule #1, but it must be emphasized. The more movement and action you put in your picture the more your mind's eye will notice it. It is similar to how we turn to look at movement in our peripheral vision. In my example above, "cheerfully and eagerly" is depicted with an abundance of action.

Rule #3   Personalize it and increase retention. If you insert yourself, a family member or a close friend in the picture, you will be much more likely to remember it. That's why I tell you, the reader, to picture yourself in most of these word pictures.

Rule #4   Exaggerate the size and number. If an insect graces your picture, make it the size of a human or even King Kong. Instead of just one insect, maybe a million would be better. Again, the kitty in "alacrity" stands abnormally six feet tall.

Rule #5   Use all five senses. If it stinks, make it reek so badly you can feel your nose hairs curl up. If it smells good, make it euphoric. If you can hear it, amplify it. Taste it. Is it bitter, sweet, sour, or spicy? If it hits you, make it really hurt...maybe it gives you a bloody nose.

Rule #6   Add color. Who says your bloody nose must be red? That is too normal and logical. You will more easily remember the impossibility of blue or hot pink blood.

The common denominator to all of these rules is "nonsensical." Anything goes with your picture. The less possible you make it, the better. The only limit lies in your imagination.

The Format

The format for this book is simple. I give the pronunciation for the word, indicate its part of speech (e.g., noun, verb, etc.), I define it, list several synonyms, and use it in a sentence. You will notice a theme with the sentences. If a sample sentence didn't immediately come to mind as I was writing, I gleefully launched a salvo into the stereotypical politician's camp. I thoroughly enjoyed goring that ox. In Volume II, I might switch it around a little and take a few swipes at another group we like to needle, lawyers.

If it involves a Latin origin, I include it. More than half of all English words stem from Latin. Interestingly, I have discovered close to ninety percent of SAT words stem from Latin. Sometimes I will give the Greek origin.

After all of the boring stuff, the fun begins. That's where I give the memory word and the motion picture, followed up with a snapshot of the motion picture, drawn by my wonderful artist Kris Hagen. On rare occasions the illustration will look more generic than the written picture I created (e.g. see idiom on page 163). Sometimes I need to do this to avoid copyright and trademark issues.

Use Your Creativity

I strive to come up with a memory word that rhymes as closely as possible. Sometimes it is a laborious struggle to accomplish this goal. Occasionally nothing satisfactory comes to mind, but I do the best I can. You may instantly come up with a better rhyme word and consequently a better picture. If so, use your own mnemonic instead of mine. If you think you come up with something better, let me know, and maybe I'll use your picture for the next edition or volume.

Have fun and look for more volumes of *Visualize Your Vocabulary* in the near future.

Vocabulary Words

edify: (ed-uh-fahy) **verb** – to instruct in moral, religious, or intellectual matters

synonyms: educate, enlighten, improve, teach, uplift

*Latin's "aedificare" means "to build, erect, construct, improve." The purpose of this book is to **edify** you and help build a strong reading and speaking vocabulary.*

memory word: egg-to-fly

picture: An egghead professor *enlightening* you on how to enable an *egg to fly*.

eschew: (es-**choo**) **verb** – to avoid, especially on moral or practical grounds

synonyms: abstain, avoid, escape, forgo, give up, renounce, shun

*Ovo-lacto vegetarians **eschew** all animal flesh. However, they are not averse to consuming animal products such as dairy and eggs.*

memory word: achoo!

picture: A tree-hugging, vegetarian type at a fancy cocktail party. A server walks up to her with an hors d'oeuvres platter filled with meat. She's offended and deliberately sneezes, *"aaaachoo"* on the tray of food, then ***turns her nose up and walks away***.

upbraid: (uhp-brayd) **verb** – criticize or scold; to reproach angrily and abusively

synonyms: berate, castigate, censure, chasten, chastise, reproach

*The manager wasted no time informing the employees of the purpose for the meeting, as he walked into the room and immediately **upbraided** them for their laziness and low productivity.*

memory word: up-braid

picture: You're braiding a girl's long hair for the first time. You try to braid her hair into a pigtail, but you're new at this, so you begin from the bottom and struggle to braid up. She spins around—red faced, with steam blowing out her ears—and launches into a tirade, criticizing you for *up braid*ing instead of braiding down.

histrionic: (his-tree-**on**-ik) **adjective** – overly dramatic; deliberately affected

synonyms: melodramatic, overacting, theatrical, thespian

Latin's "histrionicus" means "dramatic" and "histrio" means "an actor or performer in pantomime." Jan's **histrionic** *moans failed to convince the school nurse to send her home.*

memory word: his-tree-on-it

picture: An immense meteor heads for your house, threatening to demolish it. At the last second, Paul Bunyan runs up, quickly chops down a tree, and strips its limbs off. He *pauses for effect*, taps the bottom of his boots with the tree-trunk, and with *theatrical and dramatic effect* points up to the sky like Babe Ruth often did. The meteor approaches until... WHACK! He swings and smashes *his tree on it,* and sends the meteor back into space.

imperative: (im-**per**-uh-tiv) **adjective** – necessary

synonyms: critical, essential, immediate, important, urgent

*Latin's "imperare" means "to command, to order." During World War II, thousands of women served on the homefront rolling bandages, packing boxes, and pulling shifts at ammunition, and other factories. They saw the necessity of their new roles as morally **imperative.***

memory word: parrot-rib

picture: Your *parrot* with a *rib* sticking out of his side, which he keeps hanging up on things. It is *critical* you mend him ASAP! Go out to the tool shed and grab a hack saw… Hurry!

perfidy: (**pur**-fi-dee) **noun** – betrayal of a trust or confidence

synonyms: disloyalty, duplicity, treachery, treasonous

Latin's "perfidus" means "faithless, treacherous, disloyal, deceitful." Drug dealers have a natural **perfidy**. *They cannot be trusted and frequently become informants on each other.*

memory word: bird-feet

picture: You trust your neighbor to take care of your pet bird over the weekend while you are out of town. You leave and return in a few minutes because you forgot your luggage, only to find your neighbor has **bird feet** sticking out of his mouth, cheeks puffed out and feathers all around. He has clearly **betrayed your trust**.

sanguine: (sang-gwin) **adjective** – happy; reddish

synonyms: cheerful, enthusiastic, ruddy, upbeat

Latin's "sanguineus" means "bloody, bloodstained." (In medieval times they believed blood was one of the four bodily humors or fluids influencing one's attitude. People thought those with a ruddy complexion carried an excess of blood and displayed a good nature.) After every election, roughly half the voters are **sanguine** *because their candidate won, and the other half are unhappy with the results.*

memory word: painguin

picture: A stereotypical Texan wearing a ten gallon hat. Next to him, his six-foot-tall pet penguin who laughs all the time. Tex has a southern twang and calls him his *happy painguin*.

euphemism: (**yoo**-fuh-miz-uhm) **noun** – the substitution of a pleasant or inoffensive word or expression for one considered offensive or hurtful

synonyms: circumlocution, grandiloquence, pretense

*"To pass away" is a **euphemism** for "to die."*

memory word: youth-prison

picture: The distraught mother of a teenage boy convicted of a crime cannot bring herself to utter the words "**youth prison**." To describe where her son is going, she prefers to **substitute the more pleasant-sounding** "juvenile detention center."

tirade: (tahy-**rayd**) **noun** – a long abusive outburst, or vehement speech or writing

synonyms: condemnation, diatribe, harangue, screed, tongue-lashing

After listening to a **tirade** *by the communist dictator, the audience stood motionless and stunned.*

memory word: high-rate

picture: A police officer clocks you, or someone you know who habitually drives over the speed limit, doing 80 in a school zone. (I picture Pat Gray -- an admitted lead-footed driver -- of the Pat and Stu show, a humorous news and political TV show and podcast.) He pulls Pat over and gives him a *severe tongue lashing* and a citation for driving at such a *high rate* of speed in a school zone.

embody: (em-**bod**-ee) **verb** – to give a tangible or concrete form to an abstract concept; to be an example of, or express, an idea or principle; to unite in a comprehensive whole or body

synonyms: epitomize, exemplify, exhibit, personify, symbolize

*The Founding Fathers **embody** the ideals of the preamble to the Constitution.*

memory word: M-body

picture: A big, confident, chiseled letter M teaches a Mega Motivational course. He tells the room full of average Ms, "Just because you're a bunch of average, skinny letters in the middle of the alphabet doesn't mean you have to stay that way. By the end of the day, you will have the tools necessary to become like me. You, too, will ***exemplify and epitomize*** excellence and magnificence like the ***M-body*** standing before you."

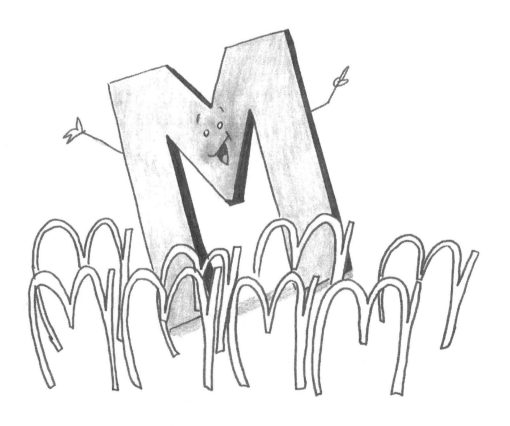

pompous: (**pom**-puhs) **adjective** – characterized by an ostentatious display of importance

synonyms: arrogant, conceited, inflated, narcissistic, uppity, vain

Some consider Rush Limbaugh to be **pompous,** *but if they would take the time to listen to his radio show instead of how the media characterizes him, they would realize his bombastic persona is part of his shtick. Off mic, he is very humble and gracious.*

memory word: pom-pus

picture: A cheerleader *filled with self-importance* is performing a cheer in front of the mirror. She cheers, "Rah rah ree, look at me. Rah rah rate, I'm so great. Rah rah razem, watch me dazzle 'em. Rah rah raisin, I'm so amaz'n." All the while, disgusting pus oozes and drips from her pom-poms. She's so focused on herself she doesn't even notice the *pom pus.*

rhetoric: (ret-er-ik) **noun** – the art of speaking or writing effectively and eloquently

synonyms: bombast, grandiloquence, oration, pomposity, verbosity

*Unfortunately, the public responds to the **rhetoric** of dishonest politicians and we seem to elect the most wretched candidates.*

memory word: Red-Derek

picture: Derek Kaczynski is a university professor, and a card-carrying member of the Communist Party. He teaches Rhetoric 101: **the art of effective speaking and writing**. In doing so, he constantly uses rhetoric to indoctrinate his students and turn them into little Communists. Every class period he gives an impassioned anti-Capitalism/pro-Marxism speech. The longer his **oration** lasts, the redder and more impassioned he gets. The students call him **Red Derek** because he turns red and for his avowed communism.

avarice: (av-er-is) **noun** – insatiable greed for riches

synonyms: covetousness, cupidity, greediness, parsimony, rapacity

Latin's "avere" means "crave, long for." Crassus, a Roman general and politician, exhibited many virtues obscured by one vice, namely **avarice***. His avarice led him to amass the greatest wealth in all of Roman history.*

memory word: a-virus

picture: *A virus* with a big mouth full of sharp teeth. He just tore the bank vault door off of its hinges and is now shoving all of the contents into his mouth. The *greedy* virus *insatiably devours* it as fast as he can. The contents? Tons of cash, gold bullion, and gold coins.

nadir: (nay-deer) **noun** – the point on the celestial sphere directly beneath a given position or observer and diametrically opposite the zenith; the lowest point; point of greatest adversity or despair

synonyms: all-time low, bottom, low point, record low, rock bottom

*The **nadir** of our annual family vacation is the last day, when we must pack up and go home.*

memory word: neigh-deer

picture: You think Rudolf the red-nosed reindeer reached his ***lowest point*** when all the other reindeer made fun of him and wouldn't let him participate in their reindeer games? Well, picture a reindeer with the face and voice of a horse. Picture this ***Neighdeer*** with his ***head hung low,*** surrounded by the other reindeer as they mock him by neighing like horses.

dormant: (**dawr**-muhnt) **adjective** – not now manifest or showing signs of activity

synonyms: asleep, hidden, inactive, inert, latent, quiescent

Latin's "dormire" means "to sleep, rest." As winter approaches, a tree's leaves begin to fall and it becomes **dormant** *until spring, when it wakes up and shows signs of life once again.*

memory word: doormat

picture: You throw a party and, as the guests arrive, they must step over the *doormat* because it is rolled up with its eyes closed. Shhhh! It is *sleeping.*

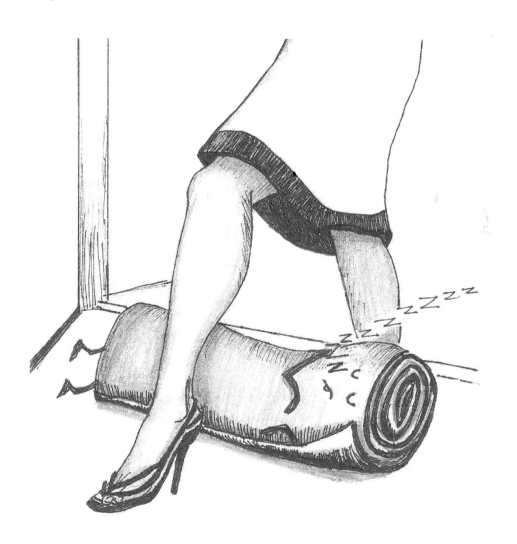

immutable: (ih-**myoo**-tuh-buhl) **adjective** – incapable of changing or being changed

synonyms: inflexible, steadfast, unalterable, unchangeable

*Latin's "immutabilis" means "unchangeable, unalterable." Physics is an exacting science, bound by **immutable** laws, which are true and fixed throughout the universe.*

memory word: a-mute-bull

picture: A bull takes a vow of silence so he is effectually *a mute bull*. You *cannot change his mind* and make him talk, no matter how hard you try.

vacuous: (vak-yoo-uhs) **adjective** – characterized by a lack of ideas, intelligence, or thought

synonyms: blank, empty-headed, fatuous, inane, unintelligent

*Latin's "vacuus" means "empty, devoid of, free of." Rush Limbaugh has a name for such **vacuous** symbolic gestures as wearing colored ribbons for various causes, or throwing frisbees for peace. He calls it "symbolism over substance."*

memory word: vacuum-dust

picture: Imagine Homer Simpson or some other cartoon character representing a big *dummy*. See yourself popping his head open with a jumbo bottle opener. Then you *vacuum dust* and cobwebs out of his otherwise *empty head.*

bedlam: (bed-luhm) **noun** – a scene of uproar and confusion; a chaotic situation

synonyms: chaos, madhouse, mayhem, pandemonium, turmoil, uproar

*When someone yelled "fire" in the theater, sheer **bedlam** ensued.*

memory word: bed-lamb

picture: You're lying in bed counting sheep, trying to sleep. The next thing you know your *bed* is full of *lambs.* They jump all over you, fighting with each other, and generally creating *anarchy and mayhem.*

utopia: (yoo-**toh**-pee-uh) **noun** – an ideal place or state; any visionary system of political or social perfection

synonyms: bliss, Eden, heaven, paradise, Promised Land, Shangri-la

Greek's "outopos" means "place." Mark Levin writes about the unattainable and futile search for a perfect society in Ameritopia. *He explains how the progressive masterminds nearly succeeded in transforming America into their concept of* **utopia**. *Hence "Ameritopia." His latest book,* The Liberty Amendments: Restoring the American Republic, *lays out a possible solution to counter the overreaching power grab of the disillusioned statists.*

memory word: u-toe-be-ah

picture: A giant letter U and big toe from Boston travel the world in search of the **perfect paradise**. At long last the best friends stumble upon it. They stand in awe of the beautiful be-ah (beer) valley before them. They see a waterfall, stream, and lake of be-ah instead of water. The trees offer low-hanging bottles of be-ah waiting to be plucked. Hop and barley fields dot the landscape. Turns out, **heaven on earth** is a **u, toe, be-ah**.

sanctimony: (**sangk**-tuh-moh-nee) **noun** – the pretense or affectation of having virtues, principles, or beliefs one does not actually have; hypocritical religious devotion

synonyms: affectation, hypocrisy, pharisaic, phoniness, speciousness

Latin's "sanctimonia" means "sacredness; purity, virtue." I can't tolerate the **sanctimony** *of one politician criticizing and besmirching the morals and ethics of another.*

memory word: Sanka-money

picture: Do you know someone who is sanctimonious? Picture him or her, or a politician, sitting in church. The offering plate comes around and this person stands up rattling a Sanka coffee can. He stole the lunch-money coins in it from neighborhood kids. He makes a *phony display* of pouring the *Sanka-money* into the offering plate. Now that is sanctimony! (Sanka was the first instant decaffeinated coffee. It's bright orange label became associated with decaf coffee by the consumer. Consequently, orange-handled decaf coffee pots made their way into coffee shops and restaurants whether they served Sanka brand or not. Businesses serving Folgers brand decaf usually have green-handled pots.)

apropos: (ap-ruh-**poh**) **adjective** – relating to the matter at hand; to the purpose

synonyms: appropriate, felicitous, fitting, opportune, pertinent, relevant

Latin's "proponere" means "to set forth, propose." Grandpa is one of those people who can remember every joke he's ever heard, and he delights in sharing an **apropos** *joke for every topic of discussion.*

memory word: app-row-pole

picture: You go kayaking or canoeing. Somehow you lose your oars, leaving you stranded out in the middle of the lake. How *apropos*, a Smartphone drops from the sky right into your lap. Even more *fitting and opportune,* it includes an app for a rowing pole. Some might call it an *app-row-pole*, others might call it an oar.

albeit: (awl-**bee**-it) **conjunction** – although; even if

synonyms: admitting, even though, notwithstanding

*I voted for my candidate, **albeit** very reluctantly.*

memory word: I'll-be-it

picture: A pirate ship floats out in the middle of the ocean, and the crew is bored to death. No wind means they just sit and wait for any puff to fill their sails so they can move on. One of them suggests they play tag, but no-one wants to be "it." A stereotypical pirate says ***I'll be it**, **even though*** he knows he is the least likely to tag anyone since he wears a peg leg, and a patch over one eye. They laugh at him and, even though they know he is no competition, they say, "You're on, peg leg."

froward: (**froh**-werd) **adjective** – willfully contrary; not easily managed

synonyms: difficult, disobedient, obstinate, unmanageable, wayward

*I never saw such a **froward** kid in my life. He simply will not behave.*

memory word: forward (pronounced *froward* by a two year old)

picture: Do you know a little boy in his "terrible twos?" Picture the little brat chasing the family cat with an enormous pair of scissors and intending to give it a haircut. His parents shout, "Stop it! Give me those scissors! Where did you get those huge scissors? Stop chasing Fluffy! Seriously, those scissors are bigger than you!" What does the **obstinate, disobedient, unmanageable** little 'precious' do? He hops on the family dog, pretending it's a horse, digs his heels into Phaedo's ribs, and commands, "**Froward**. March!"

alacrity: (uh-**lak**-ri-tee) **noun** – cheerful eagerness or readiness to respond; liveliness

synonyms: eagerness, fervor, keenness, sprightliness, zeal

*Latin's "alacritas" means "liveliness, enthusiasm, eagerness." It's fun to watch children open their birthday gifts with **alacrity**.*

memory word: a-black-kitty

picture: Your *black kitty* is quite unusual. You return home after a long day at school and your six-foot-tall black kitty, who can walk on his hind legs, ***cheerfully and eagerly*** runs out to greet you. He does a few somersaults, grabs your backpack with a smile on his face, and carries it for you. Once inside, he pulls off your shoes, puts your slippers on your feet, cartwheels into the kitchen to pour your favorite drink, and lies down at your feet purring.

eccentric: (ik-**sen**-trik) **adjective** – deviating from the customary character or practice

synonyms: aberrant, abnormal, bizarre, irregular, odd, peculiar

*Latin borrowed "eccentricus" from Greek's "ekkentros," meaning "out of the center." Most businessmen wear a regular necktie, but **eccentric** ones wear bow ties or bolo ties.*

memory word: egg-centric

picture: Sir Isaac Newton gained fame for his study of gravity. He also dabbled in centrifugal force. Picture Newton spinning a turntable while placing an egg in the center and expecting the egg to fly off the edge. However, it stays in the center no matter how fast he spins it. He says, "That's bloody *odd!*" So he places the egg on the edge of the turntable, gives it a spin and, sure enough, it rolls to the center. It stays *egg-centric* so to speak, no matter how fast he spins the wheel. To this he exclaims, "Blimey, that is most *peculiar!*"

vestige: (ves-tij) **noun** – a mark, trace, or visible evidence of something no longer present or in existence

synonyms: glimmer, relic, remains, remnant, residue, trace

*Latin's "vestigium" means "footprint, trace." I spent last summer in the Mediterranean. I saw every **vestige** of what remained of the great empires of Rome and Greece.*

memory word: vest-age

picture: Have you ever noticed portraits of famous people from the 18th and 19th centuries? A fair number of them posed with one hand inserted in their vest. Search online and you will find images of George Washington, Karl Marx, Mozart, Marquis de Lafayette et al., posing with one hand (usually the right) hidden in their vest. However, the most famous one is Napoleon Bonaparte. Picture an eccentric gazillionaire who collects ancient historical artifacts—you know, stuff even older than him. He stands in front of a mirror admiring his most recent acquisition. He paid $5,000,000 for Napoleon's vest at a private auction. The vest is aged. It is so old and tattered it is a mere ***remnant*** of its former self. In fact it looks like a fish-net vest. He strikes poses in his ***vest-age***.

inadvertent: (in-uhd-**vur**-tnt) **adjective** – happening by chance, unexpected

synonyms: accidental, unintentional, unplanned, unwitting

I felt a moment of panic when I came home from work to discover I had ***inadvertently*** *left the garage door open.*

memory word: in-a-bird-tent

picture: It's Pet Day at the park. Most people bring their dogs and cats, but a few bring their exotic birds. They set up special tents for them and take them out one at a time to show them off. Unfortunately, a cat *accidentally* sneaks ***in a bird tent*** and, well, you can imagine what happens next.

respite: (res-pit) **noun** – a delay or cessation for a time, especially of anything distressing or trying; a period of rest or relief

synonyms: breather, downtime, hiatus, moratorium, recess

Latin's "respectus" means "looking back at; consideration, refuge." Everyone in the office had worked overtime every day on a very stressful project. We welcomed the **respite** *when our supervisor brought in some coffee and bagels and told us to take a break.*

memory word: rest-pit

picture: A bunch of snakes running a marathon. Periodically they slither into **rest pit** stations along the way where they can **rest**, rehydrate, and catch their breath.

incongruous: (in-**kong**-groo-uhs) **adjective** – out of place; not consistent or appropriate

synonyms: ill fitting, incompatible, inconsistent, irregular, mismatched

*Latin's "incongruens" means "out of place." I saw General Schwartzkopf, Rush Limbaugh, Sean Hannity, Mark Levin, and Glenn Beck at an anti-war demonstration. What could be more **incongruous**?*

memory word: King-Kong-roots

picture: You're watching the Superbowl on TV. The camera pans the cheering crowd to show them doing "the wave." Sitting among the fans is something ***out of place***. King Kong! He can't stand up all of the way to participate in the wave because he sat there so long he grew roots. What could be more incongruous than a fifty-ton gorilla in the bleachers at a football game?

cynosure: (**sin**-uh-shoor) **noun** – an object of general interest or attention

synonyms: celebrity, center of attraction, central, famous person

From Greek's "kynosoura" to Latin's "Cynosura," meaning "dogs tail" the constellation we now call Ursa Minor. Although beautiful and well poised, she could go anywhere and blend in without being noticed. She debuted in a blockbuster movie and now she is a **cynosure** *wherever she goes.*

memory word: sign-on-shore

picture: You go to the beach for the day. You arrive on the sandy shore to find hundreds of people gathered around looking at something. Dying of curiosity, you work your way through the crowd to discover the *center of attraction*. What do you find? A big, bright, yellow *sign on shore*, spelling out, in black capital letters, the word "*ATTENTION.*"

heterodox: (het-er-uh-doks) **adjective** – differing from an accepted, acknowledged, or established standard

synonyms: dissident, heretical, maverick, nonconformist, unorthodox

*The Flat Earth Society is a **heterodox** group which exists to prove to the rest of us the Earth is flat.*

memory word: heater-on-ducks

picture: You know how ducks fly south for the winter? Well, not this duck. He's about as *unorthodox* as a duck can be. He's a real *maverick*. Picture a *heater on duck's* back. Why the heater strapped to his back? This *nonconformist* duck will stay put this winter. He's not flying anywhere. Picture him waving goodbye to all the other orthodox ducks flying south.

trite: (trahyt) **adjective** – lacking in freshness or effectiveness because of constant use or excessive repetition

synonyms: banal, clichéd, hackneyed, old hat, used-up, worn-out

*Latin's "tritus" means "well-worn, familiar." "Never look a gift horse in the mouth" and "An idle mind is the devil's playground" are examples of **trite** sayings.*

memory word: trite

picture: Yes, the rhyme word is the same. That's because *trite* is also the name of a species of spiders in Australia, mate. They are called "jumping spiders." Picture a classroom where you hear the same old things from your teacher. You see an Australian trite jumping from student to student. He lands on their shoulders reciting *clichés* in their ears. He's a wee little thing so he speaks into a megaphone. In an Australian accent, he says *worn-out* things: "birds of a feather flock together," "the early bird gets the worm," "don't judge a book by its cover," and "the pen is mightier than the sword."

apathy: (ap-uh-thee) **noun** – lack of passion, emotion, interest, or excitement

synonyms: coolness, detachment, disinterest, indifference

*Latin's "apathia" means "freedom from emotion, want of sensation." Too many people show **apathy** during each election cycle, hence the reelection of the same scoundrels year after year.*

memory word: apple-tree

picture: You are sitting under an ***apple tree*** when a large apple the size of a basketball falls and hits you on the head. It is made of pure gold! It rolls to a stop a few feet away and you just sit there ***indifferent*** and ***disinterested***. Where's your passion, dude?

finesse: (fi-**ness**) **noun** – skillful or clever handling of a situation; adroit maneuvering

synonyms: adeptness, artfulness, savoir-faire, savvy, subtlety

*She maneuvered her hapless opponent into checkmate with superb **finesse**.*

memory word: fin-eggs

picture: A sea of eggs. Two shark fins pop up and begin ***adroitly maneuvering*** in synchronization. You are amazed at their ***polished*** and ***artful*** synchronized swimming.

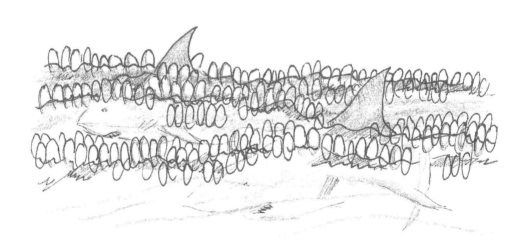

charlatan: (**shahr**-luh-tn) **noun** – a person pretending to have knowledge or ability he or she lacks

synonyms: con artist, fake, fraud, imposter, pretender, swindler

*For every ten **charlatans** elected to Congress, there is one true and honest public servant.*

memory word: sure-Latin

picture: You vacation in Rome. You stand in front of the majestic Colosseum. You see Latin words inscribed on the wall at the entrance. You ask a local if he can speak Latin and he says, ***"Sure-Latin."*** You ask him if he will read the writing on the wall to you. He says, "Yes, but it will cost five dollars." You are curious enough to pay, and hand over the money. He reads it out loud, but obviously the ***pretender*** is making it up, since he speaks Pig-Latin. He "translates" it into English, "It says, 'Latin is a dead language, so who can possibly read this nonsense?'" He calls you a sucker, laughs, and runs away. How does it feel to be ***swindled***?

ratify: (rat-uh-fahy) **verb** – to confirm by consent, approval, or formal sanction

synonyms: approve, authenticate, certify, establish, sign, validate

Latin's "ratificare" means "confirm, approve." It is my hope the Amendments, recommended by the luminary Mark Levin in The Liberty Amendments: Restoring the American Republic, *will be **ratified** as the first step to restoring the American Republic.*

memory word: rat-if-I

picture: All but one of the mice in the Mouse of Representatives are voting **to confirm by expressing consent** that rats can become citizens, too. The lone dissenter says, "Those filthy rodents! No citizenship for a single **rat if I** can help it!"

fetter: (fet-er) **verb** – a chain or shackle placed on the wrists or ankles; anything that confines or restrains

synonyms: bind, encumber, hamper, hinder, hobble, manacle, restrict

*The Founding Fathers of this great nation threw off the **fetters** of the oppressive King George III.*

memory word: feather

picture: Your hands and feet are **shackled, restraining** you. You must not be very strong because the fetters are made of **feathers**.

expatiate: (ik-**spay**-shee-ayt) **verb** – to speak or write at length

synonyms: develop, elaborate, expound, lecture, pontificate, sermonize

*Latin's "expatiatus" means "wander from the course." Uncle Bob is a walking encyclopedia. He can **expatiate** on any subject being discussed.*

memory word: X-Pace-she-ate

picture: Picture one of your teachers *lecturing* the class on the American Indians and their use of maize/corn. She walks back and forth wandering all around the area behind the podium while she *expounds* on the subject matter. A table next to the podium holds a huge X-shaped corn chip and a bowl full of Pace picante sauce. Each time she walks by, she breaks off a piece of the corn chip, dips it, and eats it. She never stops *pontificating,* so you can see the *X Pace she ate* falling out of her mouth.

bristle: (bris-uhl) **verb** – to become rigid with anger or irritation

synonyms: blow up, boil over, fume, rankle, ruffle, see red, seethe

Rush Limbaugh, Sean Hannity, Mark Levin, and Glenn Beck educate and entertain millions of people. Some **bristle** *at the sound of their voices.*

memory word: bristle

picture: You lay a paint brush down on a workbench after you're done with your project. A clump of *bristle*s pulls itself away from the others in their sticky mess. *Rigid with anger*, the clump stands up stiffly, shakes a fist at you, and shouts, "Don't you do it! Don't you dare use and abuse us this way!"

iconoclast: (ahy-**kon**-uh-klast) **noun** – a person who attacks cherished beliefs or traditional institutions; one who breaks or destroys religious images or sacred objects

synonyms: dissident, heretic, non-conformist, radical, revolutionist

Latin's "iconoclaste" means "image breaker." He reviled the status quo, but we did not think of him as a full-fledged **iconoclast** *until his arrest for vandalizing a church and city hall.*

memory word: icon-blast

picture: You are playing a video game called Iconoclast. The goal? Advance through the different levels finding icons of symbols representing **cherished beliefs and institutions**, e.g., the Statue of Liberty, the bald eagle, the United States Flag, the Liberty Bell, etc. When you click on the **icon** it **blasts** the symbol to bits.

reprove: (ree-**proov**) **verb** – to criticize or correct; to disapprove of strongly

synonyms: admonish, castigate, reprimand, reproach, upbraid

Latin's "reprobare" means "disapprove, reject, condemn." During dinner, I ***reproved*** *my children for not using their manners. After dinner, my wife reproved me for leaving my dirty plate on the table.*

memory word: the-poof

picture: Every time you do something wrong, a fairy appears and ***reprimands*** you. As quickly as it appears, it vanishes. ***Poof!***

factious: (fak-shuhs) **adjective** – given to faction; a group or clique within a larger group, party, or government

synonyms: contentious, divisive, insurgent, mutinous, partisan

*Latin's "factiosus" means "partisan, seditious, inclined to form parties." The legislature couldn't accomplish anything due to the **factious** political nature of its members.*

memory word: tax-us

picture: A growing sentiment feels our federal income tax system doesn't work. Some say the rich don't pay their fair share. Others don't like the poor not paying any taxes, yet receiving a tax refund. Picture a demonstration on the steps of the U.S. Congress. Many *groups* hold up signs espousing their suggestions for how the government should *Tax-Us.* You see the Fair Tax *faction*, the Flat Tax *group*, the Vat Tax *clique*, the 9-9-9 Tax *group*, all with their signs demonstrating and claiming their plan is the most beneficial to every American. Some demonstrators are more *contentious and divisive* than others.

tedious: (tee-dee-uhs) **adjective** – wearisome due to length or dullness

synonyms: boring, humdrum, laborious, monotonous, tiresome

*Latin's "taedium" means "wearisome, irksome, tedious." I used to work on an assembly line. Now I enter data into a computer all day. I went from one **tedious** job to another.*

memory word: T-D-S

picture: You think Tom Sawyer hated his chore of white washing that picket fence? Picture an **endless** field of twenty-foot-tall Ts, Ds, and Ss. Your job? You must paint each *TDS* without dying of **monotony and boredom**.

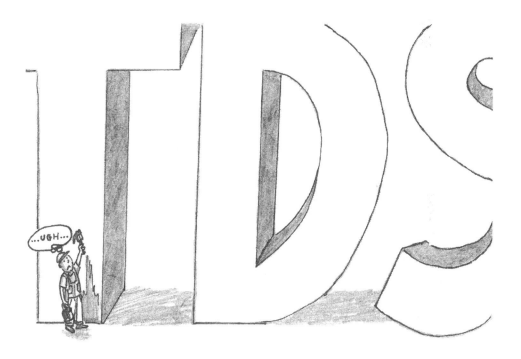

perfunctory: (per-**fuhngk**-tuh-ree) **adjective** – performed merely as a routine duty; lacking interest, care, or enthusiasm

synonyms: automatic, indifferent, lackadaisical, mechanical

*Latin's "perfunctus" means "perform, have done with." The singer performed the song so many times he lacked his usual passion and enthusiasm. Therefore, he gave a **perfunctory** performance.*

memory word: perfect-tree

picture: Everyone on your street has a tree fetish. Each year your neighbors hold a contest to see who grows the most **perfect tree** in their front yard. The same person has judged the contest for 50 years. His heart just isn't in it anymore. On the appointed day, he walks past each house and doesn't even look up at the trees. He merely **goes through the motions** and **automatically** and **disinterestedly** checks off the boxes on his **perfect tree** judging form, and saying in a monotone, "That's nice. Looking good this year."

malaise: (ma-**layz**) **noun** – a condition of general bodily weakness or discomfort, often marking the onset of a disease; a vague or unfocused feeling of mental uneasiness

synonyms: decrepitude, enervation, infirmity, lassitude, unease

*Even though President Carter never used the word **malaise** in his 1979 speech addressing our energy crisis, unemployment, and inflation, it was, nevertheless, dubbed the "**malaise** speech."*

memory word: my-laygs

picture: You're in a saloon and the fastest gun in the west comes up to you and challenges you to a duel at high noon. Suddenly you ***don't feel so well***. You feel ***uneasy, sickly***, and ***weak*** and fall to the floor. With a deep southern drawl, you say, "***My laygs***! They done give out on me. I don't feel so good."

impute: (im-**pyoot**) **verb** – credit to or blame on a person or cause; attribute or ascribe

synonyms: accredit, assign, charge, indict, insinuate, intimate

*Latin's "imputare" means "make account of, charge, ascribe." God **imputes** the righteousness of Jesus Christ to the believing sinner.*

memory word: imp-poot

picture: An imp sits on your shoulder as you stand in a crowded elevator. The little ***imp poots*** and points at you in an ***insinuating way, blaming*** you for the smelly deed.

syntax: (**sin**-taks) **noun** – the way in which words are put together; the study of the patterns of formation of sentences in a language

synonyms: arrangement, order, pattern, structure, system

Yoda provides a good example of someone who habitually uses incorrect **syntax**. *For example, "When 900 years old you reach, look as good, you will not. Hmmm?"*

memory word: ten-tacks

picture: You are the next contestant on The Price is Right. After you stop jumping up and down, Drew Carey explains the rules to his latest game. It's called *Ten Tacks*. You must push ten large square tacks imprinted with one section of a full image into a large corkboard. As you *arrange* the tacks in the right *order,* you can see the *pattern* develop until finally everyone sees the completed puzzle.

hyperbole: (hahy-**pur**-buh-lee) **noun** – obvious and intentional exaggeration not to be taken literally

synonyms: embellishment, laying it on thick, overstatement

*Latin borrowed "hyperbole" from Greek and kept the same spelling and meaning of "exaggeration, extravagance." Everything she says should be taken with a grain of salt, as she is prone to **hyperbole**.*

memory word: diaper-bowling

picture: A friend who is prone to *exaggeration* invites you to go see the latest craze called *diaper bowling*. He says the toddlers bowl while wearing nothing but diapers. You arrive and realize your friend engaged in hyperbole again. It is Peewee Bowling not Diaper Bowling. They are little kids, but way too old for diapers.

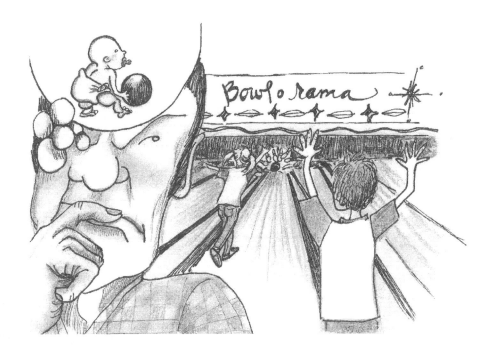

opprobrious: (uh-**proh**-bree-uhs) **adjective** – contemptuous in character or utterance; expressing scorn, disgrace, or contempt

synonyms: coarse, despicable, dishonorable, hateful, insulting, offensive

Latin's "opprobrare" means "to reproach, taunt." Alcohol, also known as the "social lubricant," makes otherwise reputable and respected people act in the most **opprobrious** *manner.*

memory word: old-paint-brush

picture: You sit on a park bench next to some jerk who feels the need to make an *insulting, offensive* comment about everybody walking by: whether their weight, posture, manner of dress, or anything different. A man wearing a toupee walks by and the *despicable* man sitting next to you says, "Well, that's a creative use for an *old paint brush*."

ubiquitous: (yoo-**bik**-wi-tuhs) **adjective** – existing or being everywhere at all times

synonyms: ever-present, everywhere, omnipresent, pervasive, universal

*Latin's "ubique" means "everywhere, universally." One of the many things I don't like about elections is the **ubiquitous** campaign signs.*

memory word: you-big-quitter

picture: A short-fused Sergeant always yells at his recruits. All Sergeants yell at their recruits, right? Picture the Sergeant shouting at a particular recruit because he can't complete an obstacle course. The recruit says, "Gahlee, Sergeant, I can't go on. I quit." This causes the Sergeant's head to explode into a million pieces. These instantly grow a million *omnipresent* Sergeant heads who all simultaneously yell, *"You big quitter*!!!"

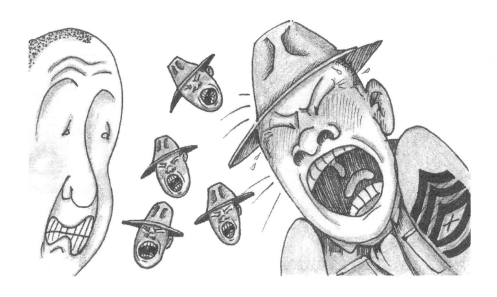

nettle: (net-l) **noun** – any plant of the genus Urtica, covered with stinging hairs; **verb** – to irritate, annoy, or provoke; to sting as a nettle does

synonyms: disturb, goad, harass, insult, irritate, peeve, pester

A guy at work never stops talking. The fact he offers an opinion about everything **nettles** *me to no end.*

memory word: medal

picture: You win a gold *medal* in the Nettle Leaves Eating Contest. You stand on the winner's podium with the medal around your neck. Your coach tells you to smile for the cameras, but you can only muster a pained look because both the *medal* and ribbon contain little stinging spikes which really *irritate* you.

remunerative: (ri-**myoo**-ner-uh-tiv) **adjective** – earning money or rewards; paying

synonyms: beneficial, gainful, lucrative, profitable, worthwhile

*Latin's "remunerare" means "compensate, reward, recoup." The transients and wanderers on Mill Avenue who prefer to beg for money consider a **remunerative** occupation as hostile and foreign.*

memory word: remove-her-whip

picture: At a wine and cheese tasting event, the host observes a wealthy looking woman facing a growing line of people. Each person walks up to this lady and holds their cheese and cracker out to her. She flicks the slice of cheese off of their cracker with her finger. When she dispenses a dollop of golden Cheese Whip on their cracker, they *pay* her with a 100-dollar bill. The host realizes how much money he could *earn* from the golden Cheese Whip if it belonged to him. So, he orders his underlings to go to her at once and *remove her whip.*

abstract: (**ab**-strakt) This word can be a noun, verb, or adjective, depending on how you use it. Also, it has about 15 nuanced definitions. We're going to tackle this word as an **adjective** – having conceptual rather than concrete existence, like an *abstract idea*; difficult to understand

synonyms: abstruse, complex, indefinite, philosophical, transcendental

Latin's "abstrahere" means "to drag away from." I just can't wrap my head around the **abstract** *concept of the universe constantly expanding.*

memory word: abs-strapped

picture: Do you know someone with a big belly? Well, for his New Year's resolution he wants to replace his belly with ripped abs. The problem is he's had his big belly for so long he can't *conceptualize* washboard abs. So, he has *abs strapped* on over his belly to help him visualize this *abstruse and indefinite concept*.

mendacious: (men-**day**-shuhs) **adjective** – habitually telling lies; false or untrue

synonyms: deceptive, dishonest, duplicitous, fallacious, fraudulent

Latin's "mendax" means "lying, deceitful." Too many politicians are willfully mendacious.

memory word: men-day-shift

picture: At the North Pole, Santa's workshop offers two work shifts. Men carry the day shift and women take the night shift. A *duplicitous*, *fraudulent*, *deceitful* female elf dresses up like a male elf so she can work the *men's day shift*.

temerity: (tuh-**mer**-i-tee) **noun** – reckless boldness; audacity

synonyms: brass, daring, gall, hastiness, nerve, pluck, rashness

*Latin's "temere" means "by chance, blindly, casually, rashly." With the **temerity** of youth, the teen drove his dad's sports car around the hairpin turns at a dangerous speed.*

memory word: to-Mary-T

picture: Did you know Stephen A. Douglas courted Mary Todd Lincoln before she married Abraham Lincoln? Well, he did. In this picture, news just arrived to Mr. Douglas announcing Mary Todd's betrothal to Mr. Lincoln. He has the *audacity* to think he still has a chance, so he *daringly* addresses a letter "*To Mary T*" to ask her to reconsider marrying him instead.

vacillate: (**vas**-uh-layt) **verb** – to waver in mind or opinion; be indecisive or irresolute; to sway unsteadily; to oscillate or fluctuate

synonyms: dither, hem and haw, hesitate, seesaw, waver, yo-yo

*Latin's "vacillare" means "to waver between two opinions or courses." Great leaders seize opportunities as they arise, they do not **vacillate**.*

memory word: tassle-8

picture: You are in charge of selecting the cap and gown colors and design for this year's graduating class at your school. The cap and gown is easy, but there are eight choices for the tassel with varying designs. You can't make up your mind on which of the ***tassel 8*** to select. Should you pick the solid color? Tri-color? Which metal trim? You ***hesitate*** and ***waver*** until you resort to choosing by eeny, meeny, miny, moe.

Machiavellian: (mak-ee-uh-**vel**-ee-uhn) **adjective** – being or acting in accordance with the principles of government analyzed in Machiavelli's *The Prince*, in which political expediency is placed above morality, and the use of craft and deceit to maintain the authority and carry out the policies of a ruler is described; characterized by subtle or unscrupulous cunning, deception, expediency, or dishonesty

synonyms: calculating, conniving, opportunist, plotting, underhanded

He became a state senator, a U.S. senator, and then President, by using **Machiavellian** *tactics.*

memory word: monkey-is-alien

picture: You attend a costume party where a *cunning* alien wears a monkey costume. It goes around lifting its mask just enough for each person to see its eyes, by which it *compels* them to quietly go outside and board the spaceship behind the building. You observe this *deceitful* alien's tactics and run around shouting, "***Monkey is alien! Monkey is alien!***"

epiphany: (ih-**pif**-uh-nee) **noun** – a sudden, intuitive perception of or insight into the reality or essential meaning of something, usually initiated by some simple or commonplace occurrence or experience

synonyms: aha! moment, inspiration, lightning bolt, realization

Latin's "epiphania" means "manifestation, striking appearance." Invention has its own algorithm: genius, obsession, serendipity, and **epiphany** *in some unknowable combination.*

memory word: Piff-on-knee

picture: You have a pile of peanuts on your knee and you slap your hand down on the peanuts. You lift up your hand to reveal a jar of Piff peanut butter. Looking at the *Piff on knee* you *suddenly realize* where peanut butter originates.

reprehensible: (rep-ri-**hen**-suh-buhl) **adjective** – deserving of reproof, rebuke, or censure

synonyms: condemnable, culpable, disgraceful, opprobrious

Latin's "reprehendere" means "hold back, restrain, rebuke." You know my opinion of politicians by now. Would you believe I think the actions of most politicians are **reprehensible***?*

memory word: rap-your-hand-against-a-bull

picture: You *rap your hand against a bull* and it bends you over its knee to punish you for your *condemnable and very bad behavior.*

extraneous: (ik-**stray**-nee-uhs) **adjective** – introduced or coming from without; not belonging or proper to a thing; not pertinent; irrelevant

synonyms: peripheral, superfluous, supplementary, unnecessary

Latin's "extra" means "outside of." We could eliminate billions of dollars in wasteful pork barrel spending every year if our representatives in D.C. would ban all **extraneous** *provisions in the bills sent to the President.*

memory word: extra-knees

picture: You are a scientific wonder because you grew extra knee caps a few inches above your normal knees. These *extra knees serve no purpose* as they are *not essential or relevant* to the function of your legs. They don't bend, but look like they could. They don't belong, but there they sit. If your current job doesn't work out, you could always join the circus!

doctrinaire: (**dok**-truh-**nair**) **adjective** – dogmatic about others' acceptance of one's ideas; inflexibly committed to putting theory into effect without regard for practical difficulties

synonyms: bullheaded, dogmatic, impractical, unyielding

*Latin's "doctrina" means "teaching, body of teachings, learning." Dad is nothing if not **doctrinaire**. His favorite saying is, "It's my way or the highway."*

memory word: Dr.-No-Hair

picture: A balding doctor is known as **Dr. No Hair** because he believes No-Hair (a hair removal product) is a panacea for every ailment. He sends each patient away with a bottle of No-Hair, no matter what malady. He is **unyielding** to the complaints from his patients about the side effects of No-Hair and its **impractical** use for acne, sore throat, eczema, etc.

juxtapose: (**juhk**-stuh-pohz) **verb** – place side by side, especially for comparison/contrast

synonyms: appose, bring together, connect, pair, place in proximity

*This year, both Groundhog Day and the State of the Union address occur on the same day. This is an ironic **juxtaposition** of events. One involves a meaningless ritual in which we look to an insignificant creature of little intelligence for prognostication. The other involves a groundhog.*

memory word: jugs-pose

picture: You open your refrigerator door to find it completely empty except for two jugs of milk *placed side by side*. One is full of chocolate milk and the other is full of regular milk. As you open the door, they come to life and begin posing to look their best for you. Each of the *jugs pose*, hoping you will pick it.

abet: (uh-**bet**) **verb** – to encourage or support by aid or approval, usually in wrongdoing

synonyms: condone, encourage, endorse, goad, incite, instigate, urge

Although they live in a very bad neighborhood, not everyone is willing to aid and ***abet*** *the drug dealers.*

memory word: a-bet

picture: You are at a blackjack table in a Las Vegas casino. You are a little intimidated and are reluctant to place ***a bet***. That's when Wayne Newton, Elvis Presley, The Rat Pack, Liberace, The Blue Man Group, Celine Dion, or some other Las Vegas icon (take your pick) saddles up next to you and ***encourages*** you to take a chance. "You only live once," he/she says.

ruminate: (**roo**-muh-nayt) **verb** – to reflect upon; to contemplate; to chew the cud

synonyms: cogitate, deliberate, mull over, muse, ponder, think

*Latin's "ruminare" means "to chew the cud, turn over in the mind." I have developed insomnia. When I go to bed I cannot stop **ruminating** about everything that happened during the course of the day.*

memory word: chew-man-ape

picture: A bunch of men and apes are *sitting* on the grass under a shade tree. They rest their chins in their hands, chewing their chow and *thinking* really hard. Maybe each man and ape wonders what the others are *pondering*.

narcoleptic: (**nahr**-kuh-lep-tik) **noun** – a person who is subject to narcolepsy, which is a condition characterized by frequent and uncontrollable attacks of deep sleep

synonyms: coma, sedation, swoon

*My friend's brain surgery took twice as long as expected because, it turns out, his surgeon is **narcoleptic**.*

memory word: narcotic-tick

picture: A giant tick pops narcotic pills and *lapses into a deep sleep*. When he wakes up awhile later, the *narcotic tick* pops more narcotics and once again *falls into a deep sleep*.

spurious: (spyoor-ee-uhs) **adjective** – not genuine, authentic, or true; not from the claimed, pretended, or proper source; of illegitimate birth

synonyms: bogus, fake, false, meretricious, phony, unauthentic

*Latin's "spurius" means "illegitimate, false." The politician's speech is littered with plagiarism, cynicism, and **spurious** facts.*

memory word: spear-U.S.

picture: You watch a documentary about Spartacus called *Sparadakos,* which means "famous for his spear." Ironically, a news alert interrupts the movie to cover a militant Islamic terrorist group's video of the launch of a massive, spear-shaped, nuclear missile on its way to the United States. Of course, everyone who sees the *"Spear U.S."* news bulletin panics. Thankfully, another news alert interrupts the broadcast a few minutes later to inform the public the Department of Homeland Security identified the terrorist video as ***not genuine***. It is merely a computer-generated, *fake* missile.

grandiose: (**gran**-dee-ohs) **adjective** – impressive because of unnecessary largeness or grandeur; more complicated or elaborate than necessary

synonyms: extravagant, flamboyant, ostentatious, pretentious

*Latin's "grandis" means "large, great, grand." Each successive Roman emperor built more **grandiose** monuments to himself than the last.*

memory word: grand-eels

picture: Poseidon throws another one of his "I'm the King of the Sea" parties. Each of these parties always grows more *impressive* than the last. Golden statues of him grow *unnecessarily larger* each time. This time, the mile-long driveway leading to his mansion is bordered by a solid pearl colonnade of 20-foot-tall *Grand Eels*.

vapid: (vap-id) **adjective** – lacking liveliness, sharpness, or briskness

synonyms: flat, insipid, lifeless, spiritless, tiresome, uninteresting

*Latin's "vapidus" means "flat, insipid, (literally, 'that has exhaled its vapor')." She can sing beautifully, but the songs she writes include nothing but **vapid** lyrics.*

memory word: zap-it

picture: You're having a bad hair day. Your hair lies ***flat and lifeless***. So, you stick your finger in the electrical outlet and ***zap it***. That did the trick. Now your hair has more body than you know what to do with. (Legal disclaimer: **Don't do it!**)

misanthrope: (**mis**-uhn-throhp) **noun** – one who dislikes, distrusts or hates other people and/or mankind in general

synonyms: cynic, grouch, grump, hater, loner, recluse, skeptic

*My nextdoor neighbor is a **misanthrope**. Signs in his front yard say, "GO AWAY" and "NO TRESPASSING." When he takes a walk, he crosses the street, rather than walk directly in front of my house, so he avoids any contact.*

memory word: miss-and-throw

picture: A *hateful, grouchy* man sits on the steps of his front porch. A pile of rocks lies next to him. When anyone walks by his front yard, he throws a rock at them. He has terrible aim so he will ***miss and throw*** until they are out of reach.

apex: (ay-peks) **noun** – the highest tip or point; the narrow or pointed end

synonyms: acme, crest, culmination, peak, pinnacle, summit, zenith

*Apex is a loanword from Latin. A loanword is borrowed from another language and it keeps the same spelling and meaning. Reaching the summit of Mt. Everest, she attained the **apex** of her mountain climbing endeavors.*

memory word: Ape-X

picture: A colossal ape competes as a contestant in the Ape Xtreme Sport games. The massive ape parachutes and lands on **the peak** of the Eiffel Tower, Washington Monument, Seattle Space Needle, or tall structure of your choice, winning this year's **Ape X** games.

limpid: (**lim**-pid) **adjective** – clear, transparent, as water, crystal or air; completely calm

synonyms: crystal-clear, lucid, see-through, translucent, transparent

*Latin's "limpidus" means "clear." When I retire, I want to buy a house on a **limpid** lake.*

memory word: limping

picture: You visit a haunted house and hear the sound of someone or something *limping*. An almost invisible man rounds the corner, and you see him take a step with his good leg and drag his lame leg. You watch him slowly *limping* by, fascinated by the *clear* view of his organs. He's not invisible, just *transparent* except his organs.

morose: (muh-**rohs**) **adjective** – having a gloomy or sullen disposition

synonyms: blue, depressed, dour, down in the dumps, glum

Latin's "morosus" means "hard to please, peevish, fastidious." I suspect she is bipolar or has a split personality, as she is either on top of the world and the life of the party, or she is morose.

memory word: more-O's

picture: Picture a depressed man sitting at the counter in a donut shop. He looks *gloomy* and *down in the dumps*. He rests his head in the palm of his hand, while dunking his donut in his coffee. He's already gone through a box of donuts, yet doesn't feel any better. The waitress comes up, refills his coffee and asks, "You want *more O's*?" He shrugs his shoulders and mumbles, "Whatever."

resign: (ri-**zahyn**) **verb** – to give up/in; accept as inevitable

synonyms: abdicate, capitulate, cede, relinquish, surrender, yield

Latin's "resignare" means "to check off, annul, cancel, give back." Far too many people are **resigned** *to an out-of-control federal government, and to politicians trampling on the Constitution. Not Mark Levin, the author of* The Liberty Amendments: Restoring the American Republic. *Read it and join the effort to restore the Constitution.*

memory word: reed-sign

picture: A sign is on the run. It hides in the reeds along a river bank. The law catches up with it and flushes it out using some police dogs. The *reed sign* comes out with its hands up saying, "I *give up*! Don't shoot!"

ascribe: (uh-**skrahyb**) **verb** – to credit or assign, as to a cause or source

synonyms: accredit, appoint, assign, attribute, credit, impute

Latin's "ascribere" means "to write in, to add or state in writing." The witty quote, "I smoke in moderation, only one cigar at a time," is **ascribed** *to the famous author Mark Twain.*

memory word: a-scribe

picture: A scribe is someone who writes books and documents by hand. Before the invention of the printing press, the profession of a scribe was very important and held a lot of status as a remunerative occupation. Picture *a scribe* sitting at his desk copying some important documents for the local magistrates. Books and unfurled parchments surround him. A big dummy walks up and says, "Now that's some purty scribbl'n. You scribble all them books yerself?" The scribe condescendingly responds, "Of course, I take the *credit* for all of this 'scribbl'n', as you so eloquently put it, you dunderheaded oaf. Now remove yourself from my presence, as I have more 'scribbl'n' to do."

credulous: (krej-uh-luhs) **adjective** – willing to believe or trust too readily

synonyms: green, gullible, naïve, swallow whole, trusting

Latin's "credulus" means "prone to believe, trustful." Apparently most voters are **credulous**. *Otherwise, how would so many suspect politicians win election?*

memory word: bread-you-lust

picture: Incredulous Man says if you eat Lotsa bread it will make you stronger and faster than him. You are so *gullible and naive* you believe him, and lust for bread. In fact, it is Lotsa brand *bread you lust*. You eat several loaves a day but, instead of turning into Incredulous Man, you become Doughboy.

languish: (**lang**-gwish) **verb** – to become weak or feeble; to lose vigor and vitality

synonyms: conk out, droop, fade, faint, fizzle out, go soft, weaken

Latin's "languere" means "be weak or faint; lack vigor." I forget to water my house plants. Therefore, they **languish** *most of the time.*

memory word: land-fish

picture: You see several fish walking around on land. When these *land fish* approach a body of water, they begin to *lose strength*. They *become weak and wobbly* until they reach a safe distance from the water. Welcome to Bizarro World.

wanton: (**won**-tn) **adjective** – something done maliciously or unjustifiably; without regard for what is right, just, or humane

synonyms: heedless, inconsiderate, reckless, unrestrained

*Animal House's Bluto shows **wanton** disregard for everyone in the scene in which he instigates a food fight.*

memory word: one-ton

picture: A *one-ton* blob lumbers down the street gobbling up everything in sight. It has *no regard for people's property, safety, or feelings*.

eugenic: (yoo-**jen**-ik) **adjective** – bringing about improvement in the type of offspring produced; having good inherited characteristics

synonyms: genetic, hereditary

*Greek's "eugenes" means "well-born, of good stock, of noble race." The Nazis are often associated with the **eugenic** movement, but what most people don't know is Margaret Sanger, the founder of Planned Parenthood, was also a dedicated proponent of the eugenic philosophy.*

memory word: huge-hen-egg

picture: You own a chicken farm. You try to grow ***bigger, better, faster*** chickens. You focus on encouraging them to lay ***huge hen eggs***. The bigger the better. You breed the biggest roosters with the biggest hens and they require a special diet.

repudiate: (ri-**pyoo**-dee-ayt) **verb** – to reject as having no authority or binding force; to cast off or disown; to reject with disapproval or condemnation

synonyms: censure, chide, condemn, denounce, denunciate, disparage

Latin's "repudiare" means "to cast off, put away, reject, scorn." Strict constitutional constructionists **repudiate** *the notion the U.S. Constitution is a "living, breathing document."*

memory word: the-food-he-ate

picture: You are at a wedding reception with assigned seating You're seated at a table next to the fattest man you've ever seen. He gobbles down everything set in front of him. He demands more food each time a server brings him a plate of food. The table is a disgusting mess and you even have some of his food shrapnel on you. You are repulsed and leave in disgust saying, "I can't believe **the food he ate**. You **reject in the strongest terms** the notion you have to sit next to him, and demand to be moved to another table. You even wag your finger at him as you **condemn** him for his lack of respect for those around him.

bolster: (bohl-ster) **verb** – to support or strengthen

synonyms: aid, assist, help, sustain, uphold

*A good friend is someone who **bolsters** others when they need help.*

memory word: bowl-stir

picture: One of your friends enters the ***Bowl Stir*** competition. Your friend must hold a large bowl of acid over her head and stir it constantly. The last one still stirring their bowl wins a million dollars! Each ***Bowl Stir*** contestant is allowed to have one friend ***assist*** by ***supporting*** his or her arms. What a good friend you are to risk getting burned by acid.

convivial: (kuhn-**viv**-ee-uhl) **adjective** – cheerful or festive

synonyms: friendly, fun-loving, jovial, merry, pleasant, sociable

Latin's "convivere" means "to carouse together." Everyone knows that special **convivial** *person who is the life of the party.*

memory word: con-video

picture: Imagine yourself as the warden of a prison. The head guard comes to you with a video of some of the convicts. He says, "Warden you gotta see this *con video*. There's something very peculiar about their behavior." You pop the videotape in, and expect to see the convicts acting tough and intimidating. Instead, you observe them slapping each other on the back, having a *merry* old time. They actually seem very *pleasant and agreeable*. The convicts on the *con video* are convivial. Go figure.

dichotomy: (dahy-**kot**-uh-mee) **noun** – division into two contrasting groups

synonyms: difference, disunion, duality, separation, split

*The **dichotomy** between the mainstream media and talk radio could not be starker.*

memory word: Psycho-Tommy

picture: You are placed in a prison cell with **Psycho Tommy**. The cell door closes, and it's just the two of you. However, Psycho Tommy informs you he's in charge of everyone in the cell. In his mind, dozens of inmates share the cell. You say, "It's just the two of us, and you're not the boss of me." To which Psycho Tommy says, "I can see you are going to be trouble, so I'm putting you over there with the troublemakers. Here's your black hat." He puts an imaginary black cowboy hat on you and tells you that's how he keeps track of the good guys and bad guys. The good guys wear white hats.

nebulous: (**neb**-yuh-luhs) **adjective** – hazy, indistinct, vague

synonyms: ambiguous, cloudy, indefinite, murky, unclear

*Latin's "nebulosus" means "cloudy, hazy, misty, foggy, vaporous, obscure." When James came to, he had a **nebulous** recollection of someone shouting "duck!"*

memory word: nephew-Les

picture: You go to a family reunion and see people you haven't seen in years. You have lots of nephews you remember, but you can only *vaguely* remember your *nephew Les*. He says, "Remember how you used to take me to ball games and take me fishing?" As hard as you try to remember these excursions with *nephew Les*, your memories of *nephew Les* are *hazy and vague*.

diffident: (**dif**-i-duhnt) **adjective** – lacking confidence in one's own ability or worth

synonyms: abashed, reserved, self-conscious, shy, timid

*Latin's "diffidere" means "to distrust, lack confidence." If you are shy, reserved, and have a **diffident** manner, professions such as motivational speaker, stand-up comic, or politician would not be a good match for you.*

memory word: different

picture: Reluctantly, you attend a dance. Everyone is unabashed and having a great time. Each person does a different dance e.g., Jitterbug, Twist, Bop, Watusi, etc. Somebody is even clogging! You, however, are *different. **Shy, timid, and self-conscious,*** you sit in the corner watching everyone who is not *different* dance the night away.

garble: (**gahr**-buhl) **verb** – to distort the meaning or sound of

synonyms: falsify, jumble, mutilate, obscure, twist, warp

*Talking with marbles in one's mouth is not only dangerous, but it also **garbles** your speech, making it hard to understand what you are saying.*

memory word: gargle

picture: You might describe your co-worker Gary as "a different colored bird." Every time he wants to say something, he takes a drink of water and gargles as he speaks. He's actually gotten fairly good at it. You can understand most of what he says even though it is a **distorted gargle**. Some avoid Gary The Gargler, but others enjoy engaging him just for the entertainment value.

laconic: (luh-**kon**-ik) **adjective** – using few words; to the point

synonyms: brief, concise, curt, pithy, succinct, terse

*Ancient Sparta was located in the area of Laconia. Its inhabitants were famously proud of their brevity of speech. When Philip of Macedon threatened them with, "If I enter Laconia, I will raze Sparta to the ground," the Spartans' replied "If." Neil Armstrong, the first person to walk on the moon, stepped off of the Apollo Lunar Module onto its surface, and said **laconically**, "That's one small step for [a] man, one giant leap for mankind."*

memory word: lick-on-it

picture: On a cattle ranch, a mother cow leads her calf to a salt block for the first time. The mother says to the calf, "***Lick on it***." The calf asks why and mom says, "Lick on it or you die." The calf insists on an explanation, but mom is very ***sparing of words*** and simply reiterates, "***lick on it***" and walks away. What her calf doesn't know and mom doesn't explain, because she is always ***concise,*** is cows need the minerals sodium, calcium, and selenium, etc., in salt or they become increasingly sick and die. The ranchers provide fifty-pound blocks of salt for them to lick. (Believe it or not, Baker City, Oregon holds an annual Salt Lick City Cow Lick art competition. They give cows salt blocks to lick, and display the resulting shapes as art sculptures, which are judged.)

recant: (ri-**kant**) **verb** – reject or disavow a formerly held belief, usually under pressure

synonyms: deny, nullify, recall, renounce, rescind, retract, revoke

Latin's "recantare" means "recall, revoke." Galileo's heliocentric theory went against the Catholic church's geocentric belief. Ultimately, the church forced him to **recant** *his theory and he remained under house arrest for the rest of his life.*

memory word: reek-ant

picture: A big ant stinks to high heaven. He has B.O. because he strongly believes ants shouldn't bathe. He says water is only good for drinking, not for bathing. However, another ant with a prodigious, supersensitive nose holds a gun to the head of the **reek ant**. He forces him to **disavow** his "no bathing" belief, or else.

feckless: (**fek**-lis) **adjective** – generally incompetent, ineffective, inept or without purpose

synonyms: feeble, hopeless, ineffectual, useless, worthless

Feckless is one of the many words I use to describe the typical politician.

memory word: fake-legs

picture: A *worthless* snake lays around doing nothing. A centipede scurries by him and a thought crosses his mind. He thinks if he had legs too, he wouldn't be so *without purpose*. So he slithers into the Panda Express nearby and steals some chopsticks. He tries to use them as *fake legs*, but he is *incompetent* and discovers the chopsticks are *ineffective fake legs*.

chimerical: (ki-**mer**-i-kuhl) **adjective** – wildly fanciful or imaginative; highly unrealistic

synonyms: fantastical, fictional, imaginary, mythical, unreal, wild

In Greek mythology, a Chimera is a fire-breathing creature composed of a lion, with the head of a goat rising from its back, and a tail ending in a snake's head. Our founding fathers believed the U.S. Constitution would not work without a moral and virtuous citizenry. To believe otherwise is **chimerical** *at best.*

memory word: kite-miracle

picture: You sit at the park on a cool afternoon. In the picturesque setting, people play Frisbee, picnic, fly kites, etc. You lie on your back watching the clouds roll by, and you see a formation of clouds suddenly morph into hundreds of kites. You watch it fly across the sky until it seems to morph back into clouds in the distance. Was it real or *imaginary*? You look around to see if anyone else noticed it, but they are all preoccupied with their sports and games. Did you witness a *kite miracle* or did your brain play a *wildly fanciful* trick on you?

parsimony: (**pahr**-suh-moh-nee) **noun** – extreme or excessive economy or frugality

synonyms: miserliness, niggardliness, selfishness, stinginess

Latin's "parcere" means "to spare, refrain from, use moderately." Though a multimillionaire, Mr. Burns is known for his **parsimony***.*

memory word: parts-of-money

picture: A *miserly* old bag lady, worth millions, hates to spend her money. Any time she buys something, she tears a small piece off of her dollar bill and hands it to the cashier. They all know her and always respond with, "You know we can't accept *parts of money*."

dejected: (dih-**jek**-tid) **adjective** – low in spirits

synonyms: despondent, disheartened, dispirited, downcast, sad

*Needless to say, after the stock market crash, many investors felt **dejected**.*

memory word: D-ejected

picture: A big letter *D ejected* from his fighter jet and parachutes to safety. The closer he gets to the ground, the ***lower in spirits*** he gets. All he can think about is the last thing his commander said, "Come back without a scratch on my new jet or don't come back at all!" Big D is ***dispirited and despondent*** because he knows he's in deep trouble with his commander and the other top guns will ridicule him.

bequeath: (bih-**kweeth**) **verb** – to leave property or money to someone usually in a will

synonyms: bestow, entrust, hand down, leave, pass on, will

Many societies throughout history customarily **bequeathed** *possessions to the oldest living son.*

memory word: bee-queen

picture: The queen bee of a particular hive is on her death bed. She knows the end is near so she drafts a will to *leave* the hive to her princess daughter. The *Bee Queen* also *bestows* her expensive BarBee Doll collection to her daughter.

fortuitous: (fawr-**too**-i-tuhs) **adjective** – happening by chance, especially a lucky chance bringing a good result

synonyms: fluke, fortunate, luck out, providential, serendipitous

*Latin's "fortuitus" means "happening by chance, casual, accidental." The company's success resulted from a lot of hard work and a **fortuitous** combination of circumstances.*

memory word: for-two-of-us

picture: I bought a case of *Two If By Tea* which automatically entered me in the *Two If By Tea* sweepstakes. I'm glad I took a *chance* because this time I *lucked out* and won a three-day trip to Hawaii *for two of us*. The kids will have to stay with their grandparents so my wife and I can enjoy a second honeymoon.

indolent: (in-dl-uhnt) **adjective** – slow or lazy; causing little or no pain

synonyms: idle, inactive, lethargic, slothful, sluggish, torpid

Latin's "indolentia" means "freedom from pain, insensibility." Any parent with teenagers knows how **indolent** *they can be, sleeping till noon on the weekends and slothfully entering the kitchen wondering when breakfast will be ready.*

memory word: end-of-lent

picture: You give up dark chocolate for lent. The **end of lent** comes and goes, but as much as you love dark chocolate, you are too lazy to go out and stock up on more. You usually eat a few morsels every day, but you are too **lethargic** to leave the house. You are pathetic.

clandestine: (klan-**des**-tin) **adjective** – done in secrecy, especially for purposes of subversion or deception

synonyms: concealed, covert, stealthy, surreptitious, undercover

Latin's "clandestinus" means "secret, hidden, concealed." What kid hasn't **clandestinely** *snuck out of bed on Christmas Eve to try and catch Santa in the act?*

memory word: Clan-destined

picture: The Communist Clan holds one of their *secret* meetings in the dark of night. Their leader gives a rousing speech on how the *Clan* is *destined* to take over the world.

munificent: (myoo-**nif**-uh-suhnt) **adjective** – extremely liberal in giving

synonyms: generous, magnanimous, openhanded, philanthropic

*This is a loanword from Latin, with the same spelling and meaning. George Washington was one of the most **munificent** of our founding fathers.*

memory word: moon-if-i-sent

picture: Imagine a world where space travel is quite common, for those who can afford it. One of the world's wealthiest gazillionaires also happens to be the most **openhanded** and **generous** person in the world. He's giving away vacations on the moon. He says to you, "Would you go to the **moon if I sent** you?"

cacophonous: (kuh-**kof**-uh-nuhs) **adjective** – having a harsh or discordant sound

synonyms: grating, inharmonious, jarring, raucous

*I don't understand what my dad means when he says my garage band could not sound more **cacophonous**, but he says it with a smile so he must mean it as a compliment.*

memory word: cow-cough-on-us

picture: You and your date attend a symphony. You expect to hear a harmonious sound from the musicians, but you hear the opposite. All of the wonderful music is drowned out by *grating*, annoying coughing. Cows are sitting on either side of you and your date, and they rudely turn their heads toward you when they cough. You say, "*Cow, cough on us* one more time and we're taking it outside!"

ameliorate: (uh-**meel**-yuh-rayt) **verb** – to make more acceptable, bearable, or satisfactory

synonyms: alleviate, improve, relieve

*I installed a misting system and ceiling fans on my covered patio to **ameliorate** our comfort on long hot summer days.*

memory word: a-meal-you-ate

picture: Back at school after Christmas vacation, you tell some friends about *a meal you ate,* which was not very tasty. You explain how you removed your spice-shaker-heeled shoes and shook salt and pepper on the food.. The extra flavor *improved* your meal and made it much *more bearable*.

predecessor: (**pred**-uh-ses-er) **noun** – a person or thing preceding another

synonyms: ancestor, forebear, former, precursor, previous, prior

*Latin's "praedecessor" means "forebear." Fortunately, I landed the remunerative job, but it was no fun fixing all of my **predecessor's** mistakes.*

memory word: bread-ancestor

picture: A loaf of Russian rye bread with a funny accent diagrams his family tree on a white board. He uses ancestry.com to research the **bread ancestors** who **came before** him. Interestingly enough, his Great Grandma Nutbutter was a fruitcake.

harbinger: (hahr-bin-jer) **noun** – a foreshadow of a future event; a sign of things to come

synonyms: forerunner, omen, portent, precursor, sign

Economists say oil prices indicate current inflation, and gold prices are a harbinger of future inflation.

memory word: car-bender

picture: A family has quintuplets. All five receive their driver's licenses and the dad lets the oldest of the five drive for the first time. He wrecks the car. Dad wonders if this is a ***sign of things to come***. Now he's apprehensive about letting the other four drive. Any or all of them could be a ***car bender***.

invective: (in-**vek**-tiv) **noun** – vehement or violent denunciation

synonyms: berating, castigation, diatribe, inveigh, philippic, tirade

*Latin's "invehi" means "to attack with words." It amazes me how much **invective** people throw at Mark Levin's* The Liberty Amendments: Restoring the American Republic *when they haven't even read it.*

memory word: infected

picture: A man scratches a mosquito bite on his arm. His wife keeps slapping his hand and telling him to leave it alone or it will become *infected*. After the eleventh slap, his frustration rises and he launches into a *vehement upbraid*. He shrieks, "You've got to be kidding me. We live in a leper colony on a quarantined island. Do you think I'm the least bit concerned about an insect bite getting infected?"

belligerent: (buh-**lij**-er-uhnt) **adjective** – given to waging war; aggressively hostile

synonyms: bellicose, combative, contentious, hostile, militant

Latin's "belligerare" means "to wage war." A schoolyard bully is nothing if not ***belligerent.***

memory word: Belle-is-your-aunt

picture: You live with your elderly Aunt Belle who needs assistance with daily living. Aunt Belle is a nice old lady, normal in every way except one. Every time she hears a bell, she starts shadow boxing and says, "I'll get you sucka." This otherwise benign old lady becomes ***combative and hostile*** every time a bell rings. What can you do? ***Belle is your aunt.*** If you don't take care of her, who will?

fastidious: (fa-**stid**-ee-uhs) **adjective** – excessively particular, critical, or demanding; hard to please

synonyms: discriminating, exacting, perfectionist, persnickety

Latin's "fastidium" means "loathing, squeamishness." My neighbor, incredibly **fastidious** *about his front lawn, reminds me of the character Hank Hill, from the animated television series* King of the Hill.

memory word: fast-city-bus

picture: Passengers on a *fast city bus* badger the driver because, no matter how fast he goes, it does not please them. The tires squeal around corners, screech to a stop at red lights, and smoke on acceleration. Yet, the *hard-to-please* passengers *demand* he go even faster.

tangible: (**tan**-juh-buhl) **adjective** – able to be touched; real or actual rather than imaginary

synonyms: concrete, material, perceptible, physical, tactile

Latin's "tangere" means "to touch; border on." Until someone can show me ***tangible*** *proof, I will continue to reject the notion aliens exist.*

memory word: handy-bowl

picture: An astronaut, during his spacewalk, does some routine maintenance on the orbiter. He holds a handful of nuts and bolts, and needs to put them somewhere to free up his hand. When a bowl floats by, he thinks he is imagining it. He reaches out to ***touch*** it to check if it is ***real*** or not. Sure enough, it is real. He says, "That's a ***handy bowl***."

burgeon: (**bur**-juhn) **verb** – to grow or develop quickly; become greater or more numerous

synonyms: bloom, blossom, expand, increase, mushroom, thrive

*History records thousands of cultures that **burgeoned** into thriving civilizations only to eventually decline into vestiges of their former selves.*

memory word: perch'n

picture: A beautiful bird perches on a phone line. Her voice sounds even more beautiful. Her singing attracts hundreds of other birds in a matter of minutes. They **become too numerous** to count and are all **perch'n** on the phone line, which weighs it down until it touches the ground.

unprecedented: (uhn-**pres**-i-den-tid) **adjective** – previously not known or experienced; happening for the first time

synonyms: exceptional, new, novel, original, unheard of, unique

*Voters elected FDR to president an **unprecedented** four times.*

memory word: impressive-dentures

picture: If you know anything about our first president, you know he started losing his teeth in his twenties. This required him to wear dentures, which false reports describe as wooden. Picture George Washington with dentures made of diamonds. Each tooth formed from a perfect diamond. No one has ever seen such *impressive dentures*. There's a *first time* for everything.

bourgeois: (boor-zhwah) **noun or adjective** – middle class of society, usually used in a derogatory manner

synonyms: average, common, ordinary, undistinguished

*Karl Marx coined the word **bourgeois** as a way to label a segment of the population he despised. He said the property-owning class or bourgeois exploited the poorer working class.*

memory word: poor-slob

picture: Pick your favorite socialist actor/actress/model. Unfortunately, most of the elite in Hollywood are admitted socialists, if not communists. Picture her at the top of a high-rise hotel in the penthouse suite. She gazes down on the masses of people, the hustle and bustle of capitalism down on the street. She looks down on the *common, average, middle class* of society saying, *"Poor slobs."*

disconcert: (dis-kuhn-**surt**) **verb** – to disturb or throw into disorder or confusion

synonyms: confound, fluster, rattle, ruffle, shake up, unsettle

*Someone who does not handle stress very well becomes easily **disconcerted**.*

memory word: KI∑∑-concert

picture: Ever attend a **KI∑∑** *concert*? Talk about disconcerting! Imagine how *flustered, confused, and confounded* your mother or grandmother would feel at a **KI∑∑** concert. The Kabuki face paint, pyrotechnic explosions, smoking guitars, levitating drum set and, of course, the flying bat demon that breathes fire, spits blood, and performs tongue acrobatics.

avow: (uh-**vou**) **verb** – to declare openly

synonyms: affirm, confess, proclaim, profess, swear

*Every witness in a trial must take an oath and **avow** they will tell the truth.*

memory word: a-vow

picture: You and your betrothed get married atop a ginormous wedding cake. The preacher turns to you to say, "You may say *a vow* now." You turn to your fiancé and ***declare openly*** to everyone in attendance your unbounded love and commitment.

sycophant: (sik-uh-fuhnt) **noun** – a self-seeking, servile flatterer

synonyms: bootlicker, brownnoser, groupie, groveler, minion

*A teacher's pet is a **sycophant** who flatters his teacher at every opportunity.*

memory word: stinky-foot

picture: Picture a sycophant you know kissing one ***stinky foot,*** then the other, of their boss or teacher. They always buy coffee for their boss or bring an apple for the teacher. Kissing stinky feet establishes a new low for him in his ***groveling*** and ***bootlicker*** role.

fallacious: (fuh-**lay**-shuhs) **adjective** – false; logically unsound

synonyms: erroneous, incorrect, misleading, untrue, unfounded

*Latin's "fallere" means "to deceive." Alchemists' belief in the possibility of turning base metals into gold or silver is **fallacious**.*

memory word: fillet-shoes

picture: You attend one of the popular magician shows in Las Vegas, and volunteer to go up on stage to be hypnotized. You shouldn't have done that because now every time you hear the word *'false'* or *'untrue'* you take your shoes off and begin to *fillet shoes*.

moribund: (**mawr**-uh-buhnd) **adjective** – near death; near extinction, not progressing or advancing

synonyms: declining, doomed, dying, expiring, fading, perishing

*Latin's "moribundus" means "dying, at the point of death." The **moribund** domestic oil industry abandoned once-thriving boom towns in West Texas and left them virtual ghost towns.*

memory word: floral-gun

picture: You shoot a floral arrangement with a special gun and the flowers quickly wilt, slumping over, ***nearing death***. Why would you do such a thing with your ***floral gun***?

stagnate: (stag-nayt) **verb** – to cease moving or activity; to become stale; to stop developing, growing, or advancing

synonyms: decay, decline, languish, rust, stand still, stifle, vegetate

*Latin's "stagnatum" means "standing water." When the government raises taxes too high and overregulates commerce, the economy **stagnates**.*

memory word: stag-Nate

picture: You and your buddy Nate go deer hunting. You spot a stag (male deer) and whisper, "There's a **stag Nate**." Both of you **stand still**, and try to remain quiet. The stag hears you and **stops moving**.

erudite: (**er**-yoo-dahyt, **er**-oo) **adjective** – possessing or manifesting unusually wide and deep knowledge

synonyms: cultured, educated, learned, lettered, scholarly, well read

*Latin's "erudire" means "to educate, teach, instruct, polish." If you've earned one or more Ph.D.s, you just might be **erudite**.*

memory word: airtight

picture: You sit next to a *scholarly* man on a cross-country flight. He proudly informs you he earned not one, not two, but three Ph.D.s. He proceeds to explain many things to you, starting with how and why the airplane cabin is pressurized and sealed *airtight*. At the end of the flight, you will either be more erudite, or bored out of your ever-loving mind.

aggrandize: (uh-**gran**-dahyz) **verb** – to widen in scope; increase in size, intensity, or number; to make greater in power, wealth, or rank

synonyms: augment, boost, enlarge, expand, magnify, multiply

Latin's "agrandir" means "to augment." Only a rare politician goes to Washington D.C. to serve the people, rather than **aggrandize** *himself with power, influence, and wealth.*

memory word: a-grand-eyes

picture: A Cyclops tires of his lack of depth perception. He constantly runs into things and bangs his head on the stalactites in his cave. So, he asks Theia, the Greek goddess of sight, to give him better vision. She grants his wish and turns his eye into a compound eye like that of a fly. He expresses great gratitude to Theia who *augmented and increased the power of* his eye. Now, with a thousand lenses all in one, he sports *a grand eyes* set.

rendezvous: (rahn-duh-voo) **noun** – a meeting or meeting place

synonyms: affair, appointment, engagement, get together, tryst

*The two young lovers share a secret **rendezvous** every day at the same time and place.*

memory word: Monday-blues

picture: If you are familiar with the sitcom *The Office,* or the movie *Office Space,* use your favorite characters for this picture. Otherwise, just envision you and your friends going back to school or work on Monday after a fun weekend. Everyone feels the *Monday blues*. So, every Monday all of you *meet* in the break room and try to psych yourselves up to start the work week.

germane: (jer-**mayn**) **adjective** – closely or significantly related

synonyms: applicable, apropos, fitting, pertinent, relevant, right on

*During her speech on exercise and nutrition, she swerved into topics not **germane** to the topic, e.g., juggling, yodeling, and the latest fads.*

memory word: you're-mean

picture: The school bully sits in the principal's office again. The principal asks, "Do you know why I called you in here again?" The bully knows why, but tries to distract him and throw him off topic by saying, "'Cause I smell funny? 'Cause you're lonely and like my company?" and such. After a few minutes of distraction, the principal says, "Everything you say is true, but not **relevant** to why you are here. The reason is **you're mean**."

intrepid: (in-**trep**-id) **adjective** – fearless in the face of something new or unknown

synonyms: bold, brave, courageous, daring, dauntless, valiant

Latin's "intrepidus" means "unshaken, undaunted." Lewis and Clark were nothing if not **intrepid**.

memory word: N-trip-Ed

picture: Picture a big letter N sitting in the school cafeteria. The biggest, toughest boy on campus is Big Ed. He walks by, carrying his lunch tray, and the N **fearlessly** sticks his foot out, deliberately tripping Big Ed. Everybody who witnesses it says, "Ooooooo **N trip Ed!**" Not very smart, but **brave**.

capitulate: (kuh-**pich**-uh-layt) **verb** – to give up or give in

synonyms: concede, relent, submit, succumb, surrender, yield

*The student would not heed the teacher's repeated requests to remove his hat in class. However, he **capitulated** when the teacher threatened to knock his block off.*

memory word: cap-insulate

picture: A bald man in a blizzard stubbornly refuses his wife's entreaty to put on his cap. When ice forms on his head and icicles hang from his ears and nose, he reluctantly ***gives in*** and puts on his ***cap*** to ***insulate*** his head.

harangue: (huh-**rang**) **noun or verb** – an intense and often protracted verbal attack; to address with a long, passionate, and often denunciatory speech or writing

synonyms: chewing out, diatribe, oration, philippic, screed, tirade

Before Hitler came to power, he would stand on the street corner and **harangue** *about the injustices of the Treaty of Versailles.*

memory word: hair-fang

picture: What begins as a polite request by the blood drive spokesman to donate a pint of blood quickly turns into *verbal abuse*. He launches into a *diatribe* at the audience for not caring enough to help out. He grows hair all over, and sharp fangs. It looks like everyone will give blood to the *hair-fang* guy, one way or another.

palliate: (pal-ee-ayt) **verb** – to ease or relieve without curing; to cover or conceal by excusing

synonyms: abate, alleviate, apologize for, assuage, mitigate, soothe

*Latin's "palliare' means "cover with a cloak, conceal." My dentist wrote a prescription for a pain killer, but told me it would only **palliate** my discomfort until she could remove my impacted molar.*

memory word: bellyache

picture: You double over with pain from a stomach ulcer. You drink a bottle of UlcerRelief to soothe your ***bellyache***. However, you know this will provide only a ***temporary relief*** of symptoms. It will take stronger medicine and a reduction in your stress level for a cure.

tacit: (tas-it) **adjective** – understood without being openly expressed

synonyms: assumed, implied, undeclared, unstated, unspoken

Latin's "tacere" means "to be silent." During my speech, I made eye contact with my instructor who smiled and winked at me, **tacitly** *telling me I was doing a great job.*

memory word: toss-it

picture: A boy on the school playground wants to play catch. He walks up to another little boy holding a ball. He holds up both hands about chest high with fingers splayed out in the universal gesture that says *"toss it."* The boy holding the ball understands the **unstated** desire and tosses the ball to the other boy.

callow: (kal-oh) **adjective** – young, immature, inexperienced, or innocent

synonyms: green, guileless, naive, puerile, tenderfoot, untrained

*The marine sergeant whipped the **callow** recruits into highly trained troops in record time.*

memory word: Jello

picture: Grandpa has fun with his grandkids. He takes advantage of their ***youth and inexperience***. He tells them if they can nail the ***Jello*** grandma just made for them to the tree in the back yard, he will give each of them a crisp one-hundred-dollar bill. After a few minutes of trying, they realize grandpa duped them.

venal: (veen-ul) **adjective** – capable of being corrupted, especially in return for a bribe

synonyms: crooked, dishonest, immoral, unprincipled, unscrupulous

*Latin's "venalis" means "open to the influence of bribes." Many politicians are just as **venal** as common criminals. They live to trade votes for money and power.*

memory word: green-owl

picture: A big, fat, **green owl** chomps on a cigar. He sits at a table in a dimly lit room counting a pile of money. A gun and a bottle of whiskey lie on the table. Everything reeks of corruption. From taking so many **bribes** and touching so much money, the bills' ink now saturates the **corrupt** owl's feathers, and he looks green.

levity: (lev-i-tee) **noun** – lack of appropriate seriousness or earnestness

synonyms: absurdity, flippancy, folly, frivolity, lightness

*Latin's "levitas" means "lightness, frivolity." Uncle Joe awkwardly tried to provide some **levity** at the funeral by cracking jokes about corpses.*

memory word: levitate

picture: A joker *levitates* above an open casket at a funeral service and *flippantly* tells jokes about the deceased.

genre: (**zhahn**-ruh) **noun** – a type, class, or category of art, music, literature, film, etc.

synonyms: classification, school, species, style

*A vocabulary book fits in the **genre** of Reference and Language.*

memory word: john-rock

picture: Michelangelo finishes his famous statue of *David*. Next, he begins a new *category* of stone-working called *john rock*. He starts with a block of marble and chisels away until it is shaped like a toilet. Get it? "john" rock?

belittle: (bih-lit-l) **verb** – to make seem unimportant or worthless

synonyms: deprecate, deride, diminish, disparage, put down, slam

Thomas Jefferson coined this word, which he meant "to make small." I don't enjoy playing chess with certain people because they habitually **belittle** *every move I make.*

memory word: bee-little

picture: A bee who is smaller than all of the other bees. He can't do as much work or make as much honey, so the other bees *criticize and diminish* everything he does. This *bee little*-ing *makes him feel unimportant and worthless*.

profound: (pruh-**found**) **adjective** – having deep insight or understanding; of deep meaning and great significance

synonyms: enlightened, heavy, recondite, serious, weighty

*Latin's "profundus" means "deep, bottomless, boundless, vast." Mark Levin's understanding of the Constitution is **profound**.*

memory word: pro-found

picture: A ten-foot tall, professional basketball player quits the team and leaves it all behind to search for the purpose of life. Picture him a year later on a mountaintop sitting next to a guru. The ***pro found deep wisdom and insight*** at the feet of this great sage.

usurp: (yoo-**surp**) **verb** – to seize or hold a position of power by force; take the place of

synonyms: appropriate, assume, displace, preempt, seize, supplant

*Latin's "usurpare" means "make use of, seize for use." One does not become a dictator without **usurping** governmental power.*

memory word: used-syrup

picture: You play King-Of-The-Mountain in the dining room. You stand on the table as king only because you pushed everyone else down on the floor. They can't move because you ***used syrup*** to glue them down.

accolade: (ak-uh-layd) **noun** – an award, honor, or praise; a light touch on the shoulder with the flat side of a sword done in a knighthood ceremony

synonyms: approval, decoration, distinction

*Latin's "accolare" means "to embrace around the neck." While I don't use a sword to show praise to my daughter when she gets all As on her report card, I do shower her with **accolades** and take her to her favorite restaurant.*

memory word: backup-blade

picture: A guy works at the Renaissance Festival. His job is to beknight kids with his sword and shower them with **praise**. The big nerd takes his role seriously. He even keeps a **backup blade**!

obtuse: (uhb-**toos**) **adjective** – lacking intellect, perception, or feeling; not sharp or acute

synonyms: dense, dull, dumb, imperceptive, insensitive, unintelligent

*Latin's "obtusus" means "blunt, dull." I've been trying to learn Latin, but I'm beginning to think I'm too **obtuse**.*

memory word: Rob-twos

picture: Remember Noah's Ark? Noah gave Rob a simple job, but Rob couldn't get the hang of it because of his *lack of intelligence*. Rob's only task was to load the boat with animals in pairs. More than once, Noah reminded him, "*Rob, twos*! Not threes, not fours!"

heinous: (**hay**-nuhs) **adjective** – hateful, odious, abominable

synonyms: evil, iniquitous, nefarious, offensive, outrageous

*The convicted killer on death row isn't the least bit remorseful for his **heinous** crimes.*

memory word: hang-us

picture: A gang of train robbers and killers live in the Old West. The sheriff arrests them, throws them in jail, and now stands them on the gallows. The preacher asks the gang leader if he wants to share any last words, to which he responds, "We're the rotten-est, evil-est scoundrels around. Get on with it and ***hang us***."

truculent: (truhk-yuh-luhnt) **adjective** – defiantly aggressive; brutally harsh

synonyms: antagonistic, belligerent, combative, contentious, pugnacious

Latin's "trux" means "fierce, wild, savage." The boys grew tired of giving their lunch money to the **truculent** *bully, so they surrounded him and said, "No more!"*

memory word: truck-you-lent

picture: You lend your new truck to a friend and he brings it back with dents all over it, bald tires, broken windows, and more. Suddenly, you feel *combative and very aggressive*. Steam comes out of your ears as you chase him with a bat around the *truck you lent*.

fickle: (fik-uhl) **adjective** – likely to change for no reason; not loyal, stable, or constant

synonyms: capricious, flighty, temperamental, unpredictable

*Suzy is a very **fickle** eater. What she likes today she may hate tomorrow.*

memory word: pickle

picture: A pregnant woman can't make up her mind about what snack she wants. She's halfway through a *pickle* when she throws it away in disgust, and pours herself a bowl of cereal.

incite: (in-**sahyt**) **verb** – to stir, encourage, urge, or prompt to action

synonyms: agitate, arouse, excite, foment, goad, inflame, provoke

*Latin's "incitare" means "to urge on; inspire, arouse." The thunder **incited** a buffalo stampede on the range.*

memory word: in-sight

picture: A "community organizer" develops a track record of whipping people up into a frenzy until they riot. The FBI maintains surveillance on him, and discovers he is up to it again. He stands on a college campus, ***agitating and provoking*** a group of students to take over the campus and occupy it until the school meets their demands. The FBI keeps him ***in sight***, at the ready to swoop in and grab him.

tentative: (ten-tuh-tiv) **adjective** – not definite or positive; not a fully developed plan

synonyms: contingent, indefinite, not final, provisional, undecided

*Latin's "tentare" means "to try; make an attempt." My appointments with my clients remained **tentative** until I knew definitively whether or not the court selected me as a juror.*

memory word: tend-to-give

picture: You are a very giving person and share a large amount of your income with a variety of charities. A charity solicits you for a donation of a specified amount. You say, "I **tend to give** a certain amount, but it fluctuates. It is never the same because I'm paid on commission, so my income stays **contingent** on a lot of factors out of my control. So I **never know definitively** what my income will be month-to-month."

zenith: (zee-nith) **noun** – the highest point or state

synonyms: apex, apogee, climax, height, pinnacle, summit

The goal of every pro-athlete is to retire at the **zenith** *of his career, before his performance declines.*

memory word: tennis

picture: Picture yourself at the **highest point** of the Empire State Building. You drop off the top a **tennis** ball the size of a beach ball, just to see how high it will bounce. You do this when the sun rises to its **zenith** or **highest point**. Now you can check it off of your bucket list.

beck: (bek) **noun** – a gesture used to signal, summon, or direct someone

synonyms: motion, nod, wave

*This word is almost always used in conjunction with "call." The spoiled brat expected his mom to remain at his **beck** and call.*

memory word: Beck (Glenn Beck)

picture: Glenn Beck, a radio and television host, delivers a very funny and entertaining program. However, it also has its solemn moments when *Beck* gets emotional. During a touching monologue, *Beck nods* to his broadcast partners Pat, Stu, and Jeffy. This *signal* indicates he's about to cry, and one of them needs to bring a box of tissues.

inscrutable: (in-**skroo**-tuh-buhl) **adjective** – incapable of being investigated or analyzed; not easily understood

synonyms: enigmatic, impenetrable, inexplicable, mysterious

*The professional poker player who masters the **inscrutable** poker face does not need to hide behind shades or hoods.*

memory word: tin-screwed-to-bull

picture: A rancher goes out to start his day and discovers a sheet of *tin screwed to bull* on both sides. This is completely *mysterious* to him. He walks around the bull several times, not believing what he sees. He scratches his head, *not understanding* who, how, or why this happened.

parity: (par-i-tee) **noun** – equality in amount, status, or character

synonyms: agreement, balance, closeness, equivalence, par

*Latin's "paritas" means "equality." The **parity** of the teams in the NFL is demonstrated on the field every Sunday this football season.*

memory word: parrot-tea

picture: A parrot shares the last of her tea with her husband and wants to share equally. So, she concentrates as she tries to pour the tea in *equal amounts*. This *parrot tea* will be shared in parity.

atrophy: (a-truh-fee) **noun** or **verb** – a wasting or withering away; degeneration, decline, or decrease from disuse

synonyms: deterioration, diminution, disintegration

Greek's "atrophia" means "a wasting away." Any bodybuilder will tell you **atrophy** *begins within weeks of ceasing their weightlifting.*

memory word: a-trophy

picture: You won a bodybuilding contest last year. You stopped training, let yourself go, and didn't give yourself enough time to get in shape for this year's competition. So, a lot of your muscle mass *wasted away*. Congratulations! You win *a trophy* for *deteriorating* the most since last year. Ouch!

yore: (yohr) **noun** – times past; long ago

synonyms: days gone by, good old days, olden days, yesteryear

Nantucket, the whaling industry capital of **yore**, *serves as a tourist destination today.*

memory word: door

picture: A modern-day cowboy lives in a house with a very rustic décor. All of the doors are vintage saloon doors of **times past**, even the front **door**.

nuance: (**noo**-ahns) **noun** – subtle distinction or variation

synonyms: degree, gradation, hint, refinement, shading, tinge

*A really good aroma therapist can detect the **nuances** of different brands of the same essential oil.*

memory word: new-wands

picture: A tooth fairy obtains a couple of ***new wands***. They look very similar, with only ***slight variations*** from the old ones.

engender: (en-**jen**-der) **verb** – to produce, cause, or give rise to

synonyms: bring about, create, develop, foment, generate, spawn

*Latin's "ingenerare" means "to implant, produce." The United Nations **engenders** optimism and respect, only to the world's dictators.*

memory word: engine-dirt

picture: An auto mechanic can't start a car. When he cranks the starter, he notices a cloud of dust emitting from the tailpipe. He takes the engine apart in search of the *cause* of this strange phenomenon. He scratches his head when he discovers what *produces* the cloud of dust. The pistons are full of dirt! He calls all the other mechanics over to look because none of them have ever seen *engine dirt*.

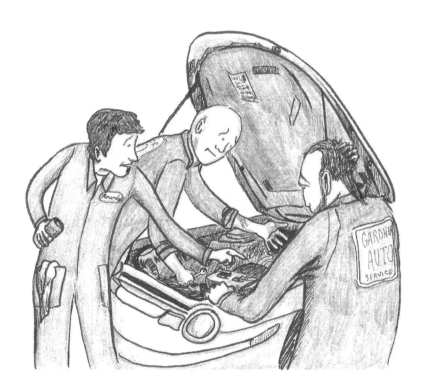

recalcitrant: (ri-**kal**-si-truhnt) **adjective** – resistant to discipline; not obedient or compliant

synonyms: contrary, defiant, froward, insubordinate, intractable

Latin's "recalcitrare" means "to be disobedient; be inaccessible." The teacher reprimanded the **recalcitrant** *student time after time.*

memory word: brick-house-in-front

picture: A *contrary* little boy removes the walkway pavers leading to the front door of his house. He wants to build a play ***brick house in front,*** right in the driveway. His dad chastises him, and makes him disassemble it and replace the pavers. An hour later, his dad checks on him and the ***disobedient*** boy has added on a room to the little ***brick house in front.***

scintilla: (sin-til-uh) **noun** – a minute particle

synonyms: iota, smidgen, spark, speck, spot, trace, whiff, whit

*Latin's "scintilla" means "particle of fire, spark, glittering speck, atom." The vast majority of politicians do not have a **scintilla** of morals, ethics, or honor.*

memory word: scent-pillow

picture: Did you know Abraham Lincoln used a hop pillow to help him sleep? Throughout history people have used hops and essential oils as sleeping aids. Picture you or someone you know treating insomnia with an essential oil *scent pillow*. Essential oils are very strongly concentrated, so you need only a *small drop* or *smidgen*.

indict: (in-**dahyt**) **verb** – to charge with an offense or crime; accuse of wrongdoing

synonyms: accuse, castigate, criticize, impeach, incriminate

*Latin's "indictare" means "to declare, proclaim in writing." They **indicted** the senator for stealing and defacing the campaign signs of his opponent.*

memory word: in-tight

picture: A mob boss and a politician are ***in tight*** together in criminal activity. They are ***accused***, tried, and convicted of their crimes. Now they share a tight prison cell.

heuristic: (hyoo-**ris**-tik) **adjective** – helping to learn; guiding in discovery or investigation

synonyms: analytical, investigative, probing, questioning, Socratic

Heuristic refers to experience-based techniques for problem solving, learning, and discovery, e.g., rule of thumb, educated guess, common sense, trial and error, and the Socratic Method, of course.

memory word: here's-your-stick

picture: Merlin the magician hands you a magic wand and says, *"Here's your stick*. Simply touch any object you want to learn about and a hologram will project from it and instruct you with facts *to help learn* about it."*

abdicate: (ab-di-kayt) **verb** – to formally or definitively renounce or relinquish a throne, right, power, claim, responsibility, etc.

synonyms: abandon, quit, repudiate, resign

*Latin's "abdicare" means "to renounce, disavow, reject." King Edward VIII of England **abdicated** the throne in 1936.*

memory word: grab-the-bait

picture: A King in all of his regalia. He decides he wants to **step down from the throne** and all of the responsibilities of ruling a kingdom. So, he takes off his crown and purple robe, **grabs the bait** and a fishing pole, and announces to his court, "I'm going fishing."

nondescript: (non-di-**skript**) **adjective** – not easily described; undistinguished

synonyms: featureless, ordinary, unexceptional, unremarkable

*Authorities recommend wearing **nondescript** clothing and using ordinary luggage while traveling, as added safety measures.*

memory word: nun-the-script

picture: You make a movie. Its concept isn't fully developed yet, so you don't write much of a script. You do know you want it to be about nuns. You hand a ***nun the script*** and ask her to read some of it. She asks what the movie is about and you say, "It's ***hard to describe***. Just read the script."

obloquy: (**ob**-luh-kwee) **noun** – censure, blame, or abusive language aimed at a person, especially by numerous persons or by the general public

synonyms: calumny, defamation, disgrace, humiliation, vituperation

Latin's "obloqui" means "to speak against, contradict." The congressman is the object of great **obloquy** *from the large group of protestors.*

memory word: odd-ducky

picture: A gaggle of other ducks surrounds an *odd ducky*. They *verbally abuse* him until he cries.

plausible: (**plaw**-zuh-buhl) **adjective** – having an appearance of truth or reason

synonyms: believable, conceivable, credible, reasonable

*Latin's "plausibilis" means "worthy of applause, acceptable." It is not **plausible** to expect compromise and solutions from the Republicans and Democrats in D.C.*

memory word: claws-on-a-bull

picture: In your dreams, everything is *believable*. You experience a dream in which *claws on a bull* are totally *conceivable*. Your pet bull rips your couch and other furniture to shreds with his claws. What's wrong with you? Everyone knows clawed bulls are outside pets.

redoubtable: (ri-**dou**-tuh-buhl) **adjective** – causing fear; arousing dread; commanding or evoking respect

synonyms: awesome, brave, fearsome, formidable, valiant

*Once the tribes merge on Survivor, one **redoubtable** contestant usually dominates the challenges and wins the individual immunity time after time.*

memory word: read-out-in-full

picture: The dictator Sulla and some subsequent Roman Emperors and other countries' dictators such as Stalin, Saddam Hussein, Fidel Castro, etc., eliminated their opponents with a political tool called Proscription. They created a list of everyone considered an enemy of the state, then murdered and confiscated the wealth of everyone on that list. Picture Fidel Castro ordering one of his henchmen to read the names on the proscription list in the public square. The dictator says, ***"Read out in full."*** Everyone listening experiences ***dread and fear, afraid*** to hear their name.

nefarious: (ni-**fair**-ee-uhs) **adjective** – very wicked or villainous; highly reprehensible in character, nature, or conduct

synonyms: abominable, atrocious, criminal, evil, heinous

*Latin's "nefarious" means "wicked, abominable, impious." The career politician left a long trail of **nefarious** acts eventually leading to his arrest and conviction.*

memory word: the-fairy-bus

picture: A *very wicked* man tells a story to some wide-eyed children gathered at his feet. Rather than a pleasant and happy story, he tells of *the fairy bus* filled with *evil* tooth fairies. Instead of leaving money under the sleeping children's pillows, they each wield a big pair of pliers to pull out the rest of the children's teeth.

innate: (ih-**nayt**) **adjective** – existing since birth

synonyms: congenital, hereditary, inborn, inherent, intrinsic

*Latin's "innasci" means "to be born in, originate in." Great leaders are not made. They are born with **innate** leadership abilities.*

memory word: an-ape

picture: You have a birthmark on your forehead. It is black, covered with hair, and in the shape of *an ape*. It has *existed since birth*.

exalt: (ig-zawlt) **verb** – to raise in rank, honor, power, character, or quality; to praise

synonyms: acclaim, boost, commend, glorify, laud, promote

*Latin's "exaltare" means "to raise, elevate." "Be **exalted**, O God, above the heavens; let your glory be over all the earth." (Psalms 57:5)*

memory word: egg-salt

picture: You hold a boiled ostrich egg in one hand and a shaker full of high-quality, expensive sea salt in the other. You *raise* both high overhead and *give praise* saying, "This is much better than ordinary *egg*s and *salt*."

lampoon: (lam-**poon**) **verb** – to mock, ridicule, or parody

synonyms: caricature, roast, satirize

On Saturday Night Live there are no sacred cows, everyone and everything is lampooned.

memory word: baboon

picture: You have a pet *baboon* which *mocks* everything you do. After it *ridicules* you, it points at you and laughs.

cajole: (kuh-**johl**) **verb** – to persuade by flattery or promises

synonyms: butter up, coax, con, entice, massage, soften, stroke

A very successful office manager keeps a lot of tricks up her sleeves to wring the most productivity out of her employees, including her favorite: "cajoling."

memory word: the-jolt

picture: A cowboy leans on a fence, about to light a cigarette dangling from his lips. A cow tries to *persuade* him not to smoke the cigarette, but he doesn't succumb to her *coaxing*. So, as he lights the cigarette, she gives him a poke with a cattle prod, sending *the jolt* of electricity running through his body.

listless: (**list**-lis) **adjective** – showing little or no interest in anything

synonyms: apathetic, enervated, indifferent, lackadaisical, lifeless

*Hospitals are filled with sick and dying patients who are **listless**, too tired or apathetic to get up and around.*

memory word: list-less

picture: Do you know a couch potato? Picture him relaxing on the couch watching TV. The show ends, and he takes another look at his list of chores. The more he looks at the **list** the **less** interest he has in doing anything on it. He decides to watch another show or take a nap.

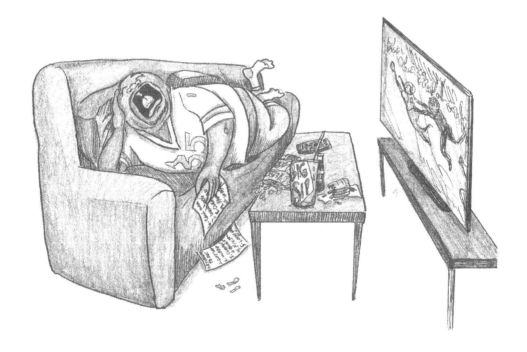

refute: (ri-**fyoot**) **verb** – to prove to be false or erroneous

synonyms: contradict, discredit, disprove, invalidate, repudiate

*Latin's "refutare" means "to drive back, disprove, repel, oppose." For every study contrived to prove man-made global warming, ten studies **refute** it.*

memory word: reef-mute

picture: An urban myth talks about a certain reef off the coast where you vacation on spring break. If you touch the reef in any way, the myth warns that you will become a mute. You swim out to the reef, touch it, swim back, and say to your friends on the beach, "Well, I just **disproved** the whole '*reef mute*' myth!"

bucolic: (byoo-**kol**-ik) **adjective** – of or pertaining to an idealized rustic rural life; of or pertaining to shepherds

synonyms: agrarian, countrified, pastoral, rural, rustic

*Latin's "bucolicus" means "pastoral, rustic." The Greek poet Theocritus lived around 270 B.C. He wrote the Bucolics, in which he praised the beauty and virtue of the rural lifestyle. I look forward to spending retirement in a **bucolic** setting, living on a small ranch, raising a few cows and sheep, and such.*

memory word: view-cow-lick

picture: Your parents spend the weekend at the *rustic* Hidden Horse Bed & Breakfast. Through every window, your mom *views a cow lick*ing its baby to give it a bath. She thinks this is the cutest *rural* scene ever. Your dad says, "You wanted to escape the rat race and experience *country life*. How do you like it so far?" She simply sighs.

wary: (**wair**-ee) **adjective** – being on one's guard against danger

synonyms: careful, cautious, guarded, leery, vigilant, watchful

*Living on the outskirts of Phoenix in a bucolic community, I am **wary** of rattlesnakes.*

memory word: wiry

picture: A Navy Seal team on a rescue mission enters the enemy camp attempting to rescue hostages, but must maneuver around many trip wires and other obstacles. Needless to say they are very *cautious and vigilant* due to the danger surrounding them. They must move very *carefully* in this dangerous *wiry* environment, or be blown to bits.

idiom: (**id**-ee-uhm) **noun** – a manner of speaking; a way of expressing oneself; a language, dialect, or style of speaking characteristic of a specific group of people

synonyms: colloquialism, expression, jargon, lingo, vernacular

*Latin's "idioma" means "a peculiarity in language." Many military **idioms** have made it into common parlance, e.g., "bite the bullet," "rank and file," and "scuttlebutt."*

memory word: idiot

picture: An annoying *idiot* goes around mimicking Homer Simpson and other *Simpsons* characters, by repeating the ***expressions and catchphrases specifically characteristic*** to the show. Some examples follow: "D'oh!," "Don't have a cow man!," "Excellent!" and "Mmmm…beer!"

abbreviate: (uh-**bree**-vee-ayt) **verb** – to shorten a word or phrase by omitting letters; to reduce something in length or duration

synonyms: abridge, compress, cut short, summarize, trim

*Latin's "abbreviare" means "to shorten; to cut off." CliffsNotes are study guides that condense or **abbreviate** versions of classics such as* To Kill a Mockingbird *and* The Great Gatsby.

memory word: a-brie-V8

picture: You gather together with your friends each week for dinner. Everyone takes turns hosting. It's your turn and you serve a blender full of Brie and V8 juice you call *a brie V8*. They tentatively take one sip of this sludge, look at their watches, and start making excuses for why they must *cut it short*. You're left sitting alone wondering why everyone scrammed and *abridged* dinner.

lull: (lull) **verb** – to put to sleep or rest by soothing means; to give or lead to feel a false sense of safety

synonyms: abeyance, becalm, calm, letup, settle, silence

*I lay in a hammock in the shade of a palapa, and allowed the lapping of the waves on the beach to **lull** me to sleep.*

memory word: dull

picture: A *dull* guy gives a *dull* speech to his wailing triplets. His voice sounds so monotonous it ***relaxes and calms*** them in no time.

bemused: (bih-**myoozd**) **adjective** – bewildered or confused

synonyms: addled, befuddled, perplexed, puzzled, stupefied

*I loved watching Looney Tunes cartoons as a kid, seeing Yosemite Sam, Wile E. Coyote, and other characters getting knocked senseless and **bemused**.*

memory word: bee-mooed

picture: You stop at an intersection, and a gigantic bee pulls up next to you in his 69 Dodge Super Bee. He sticks his head out of the window and moos like a cow. The light turns green and he drives off leaving you sitting there **bewildered and confused** wondering why a **bee mooed** at you.

rancorous: (**rang**-ker-uhs) **adjective** – full of or marked by resentment

synonyms: acrimonious, bitter, grudging, hateful, hostile

*Question a politician's judgment at a town hall meeting and watch how fast he or she becomes **rancorous**.*

memory word: rain-curse

picture: Your *hostile* neighbor washes his new car in the driveway. It clouds up, threatening to rain, so he hurries to finish up so he can pull into the garage. A sudden burst of rain catches him off guard and soaks his sparkling new car. This sends him into a *hateful* rant in which he curses the rain. You and your neighbors work outside on your lawns, but everyone rushes inside to escape, not so much the rain, but the offensive language and *hostile attitude* of his *"rain curse."*

anecdote: (an-ik-doht) **noun** – a short, (usually amusing) story

synonyms: narrative, reminiscence, sketch, tale, yarn

*I love hearing grandpa's **anecdotes** about growing up before TV, radio, computers, phones, and other technology.*

memory word: attic-rope

picture: Several, small, coiled-up ropes lie near a larger rope in a ranch-house attic. The larger ***attic rope*** tells ***short stories*** to the smaller ropes about all the things he was used for, back in the good ol' days.

allude: (uh-**lood**) **verb** – to refer casually or indirectly, usually followed by "to"

synonyms: hint, imply, insinuate, intimate, suggest

*Latin's "alludere" means "to play, sport, joke, jest." The defense attorney reminded his client not to **allude** to any matter not yet admitted into evidence.*

memory word: owl-rude

picture: You meet an owl at a party. He *indirectly* asks you rude personal questions. For instance, he wants to know how much money you make and how much you are worth, but he doesn't just come out and ask. He *hints* by asking, "If I had the same job you as you, how much of an income would I pull in?" That *owl* is *rude*.

irony: (**ahy**-ruh-nee) **noun** – the humorous or mildly sarcastic use of words to convey a meaning that is the opposite of its literal meaning; an outcome of events contrary to what was or might have been expected

synonyms: incongruity, sarcastic, satire, twist

*Latin's "ironia" means "dissimulation, assumed ignorance." My neighbor can speak twelve languages fluently. The **irony** is, he didn't utter his first word until the age of four.*

memory word: iron-knee

picture: A former militant and litigious atheist who once sued to remove God from public schools and other government entities, converts to Christianity. He now spends most of his time on his knees in prayer. He earns the nickname *iron knees*. He even wins the Iron Knees award from the American Christian Association.

enervate: (en-er-vayt) **verb** – to deprive of force or strength; to render ineffective

synonyms: debilitate, exhaust, fatigue, paralyze, vitiate, weaken

*Latin's "enervare" means "to weaken; deprive of vigor." Most people hate public speaking. Some, like me, are completely **enervated** by it.*

memory word: innard-tape

picture: A tapeworm snuggles in your innards (internal organs and intestines). He feeds on all the food and drink you consume before you can metabolize it and use it to fuel your body. This ***innard tape*** leaves you ***deprived of energy and strength***.

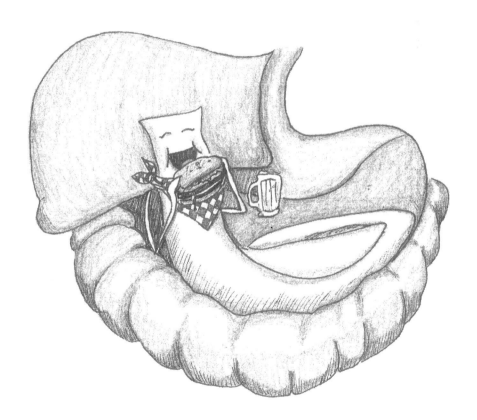

circuitous: (ser-**kyoo**-i-tuhs) **adjective** – not direct; roundabout

synonyms: long way around, meandering, oblique, rambling

Latin's "circuitus" means "encircle, surround." The Senator never answers a simple question directly. Instead, she beats around the bush and takes the long **circuitous** *route, hoping everyone will forget the original question.*

memory word: sure-cute-to-us

picture: The *Roundabout* twins, Lisa and Liza, have a crush on the *Meander* twins, Shawn and Shane. They send a friend to deliver a note saying, "You're **sure cute to us,**" **indirectly** telling Shawn and Shane "We like you, ask us out."

florid: (**flawr**-id) **adjective** – elaborately or excessively ornamented; reddish, ruddy, rosy

synonyms: decorative, embellished, flamboyant, flowery, ornate

*Latin's "floridus" means "flowery, in bloom." She writes with youthful enthusiasm and an amazing **florid** style.*

memory word: floor-it

picture: You pull an ***elaborately ornamented*** float in a parade. A hijacker jumps into your truck, points a gun at you, and orders you to ***floor it***! You put the pedal to the metal and go so fast all of the flowers blow off of the float.

hackneyed: (hak-need) **adjective** – overfamiliar through overuse; repeated too often

synonyms: banal, clichéd, commonplace, stale, trite, worn-out

*Dexter's mind started turning when he heard the killer evaded conviction due to the **hackneyed** defense of "temporary insanity."*

memory word: hat-knee

picture: Some old men sit on a park bench. One of them habitually takes off his hat and places it on his knee. As he talks, he gets animated, slaps his **hat knee** and says, "If that don't beat all." His hat becomes worn out and misshaped because this has been **repeated too often**.

ponderous: (**pon**-der-uhs) **adjective** – having great mass, weight, and unwieldiness; slow and laborious because of weight; dull and labored

synonyms: awkward, clumsy, cumbrous, lumbering, weighty

Latin's "ponderosus" means "of great weight; full of meaning." The Constitution calls for a small, unencumbered federal government, but what we built is a ***ponderous****, bureaucratic nightmare.*

memory word: pawn-dress

picture: A chess pawn wears a dress made of sponge and soaked with water. This makes the pawn's moves *slow and labored because of the weight* of the dress. The *pawn dress* is *burdensome and cumbrous*.

confound: (kon-**found**) **verb** – to confuse or perplex; cause to be unable to think clearly; mistake one thing for another

synonyms: baffle, bewilder, discombobulate, dumbfound, nonplus

*Latin's "confundere" means "to confuse; literally, to pour together, mix, mingle." The 75,000-page federal tax code **confounds** even the best CPAs, let alone the average taxpayer.*

memory word: con-found

picture: A convict breaks out of prison in New York. One hour later the police in California find someone matching the description. The police are *confused and perplexed* because they know he can't possibly travel across the country in one hour, but they hold him in handcuffs. Shortly thereafter, they discover the *con found* was not a con at all, but the con's twin brother. Talk about a *mix up*.

kindle: (**kin**-dl) **verb** – to catch fire; cause to start burning; to call forth emotions or feelings

synonyms: blaze, ignite, inflame, set alight

Hearing our national anthem **kindles** *the spirit of patriotism in my heart every time.*

memory word: Kindle

picture: You read a steamy romance novel called *Two Hearts Ignite* on your new **Kindle** Fire HDX e-reader. It spontaneously combusts, *catches fire,* right in your hands.

deleterious: (del-i-**teer**-ee-uhs) **adjective** – capable of causing harm

synonyms: damaging, destructive, injurious, nocuous, pernicious

*Latin's "deleterius" means "noxious." Everything in moderation. Too much of a good thing can prove **deleterious** to one's health.*

memory word: Dale-has-teary-eyes

picture: A bully punches Dale in the nose. ***Dale has teary eyes*** and a broken nose. That bully is definitely ***capable of causing harm*** to other kids, just ask poor Dale.

vindicate: (**vin**-di-kayt) **verb** – to clear of accusation, blame, suspicion, or doubt; to show to be right by providing proof; to maintain, uphold, or defend against opposition

synonyms: absolve, acquit, disprove, exculpate, exonerate

*Latin's "vindicare" means "to clear from censure or doubt." The defendant was **vindicated** upon the introduction of new evidence proving his innocence.*

memory word: pin-to-Kate

picture: On the second day of school, a student accuses Kate of stealing her backpack. She tries to *pin* it *to Kate*, but the next day, Kate *clears herself of blame* when she shows her receipt for the backpack.

integrity: (in-teg-ri-tee) **noun** – adherence to moral and ethical principles; soundness of moral character; the state of being whole, entire, or undiminished

synonyms: honest, honor, principled, probity, uprightness, virtue

Latin's "integritas" means "soundness, wholeness, blamelessness." Show me a politician who makes promises on the campaign trail and does not keep them, and I'll show you a politician lacking **integrity.**

memory word: nitty-gritty

picture: Abraham Lincoln sits on the witness stand for his swearing-in ceremony. The court clerk says, "Do you solemnly swear the evidence you give to the court will be the truth, the whole truth, and nothing but the truth?" Mr. Lincoln says, "Of course, I'm **Honest** Abe." A lawyer approaches and says, "Okay, let's get down to the **nitty gritty** details of this case."

despondent: (dih-**spon**-duhnt) **adjective** – feeling or showing profound hopelessness, dejection, discouragement, or gloom

synonyms: despairing, dispirited, downcast, forlorn, morose

Latin's "despondere" means "to give up, lose heart, resign." In a slow economy, many people find themselves unemployed and, if they go too long without finding a job, they become **despondent**.

memory word: this-pond-ant

picture: An ant rests on a leaf when a gust of wind blows the leaf onto a pond. ***This pond ant*** gets blown to the other bank. The ant feels ***hopeless and depressed***, wondering how he will ever make it back home way across the pond.

ephemeral: (ih-**fem**-er-uhl) **adjective** – lasting a very short time; lasting one day; anything short-lived such as certain insects

synonyms: brief, fleeting, momentary, temporary, transient

*One successful way to fight graffiti is to ensure its presence is **ephemeral**. Paint over it within a day or two or it just invites more of the same.*

memory word: if-em-er-all

picture: Your family is backpacking into the wilderness for a vacation. You cross paths with an Old Timer. He's coming back to civilization to resupply, and you are escaping it for a week. He says, "***If em er all*** the food and water you got, you ***won't last more'n a day*** or two."

mundane: (muhn-**dayn**) **adjective** – of or pertaining to this world or earth as contrasted with heaven; common or ordinary

synonyms: banal, earthly, humdrum, routine, worldly

*Latin's "mundanus" means "belonging to the world." All of my neighbors travel often to exciting places, while I live my **mundane** life and house sit for them while they are gone.*

memory word: Monday

picture: Your weekends are eventful and adventurous, filled with hiking, all kinds of sports, and traveling. *Monday* is always the same old *routine* of school, homework, and chores.

querulous: (kwer-uh-luhs) **adjective** – full of complaints

synonyms: cantankerous, grouchy, hard to please, petulant

Latin's "querulus" means "full of complaining." I thought the flight would never end. I sat next to the most querulous person.

memory word: squirrel-less

picture: Acorns weigh down a tree. It turns *grouchy* because of the extra weight and *complains* to the squirrels in a nearby tree that it is *squirreless*. Would they quit delaying and start removing its acorns? It says, "I'm not that *hard to please*. I just need you to come take a load off of my branches before I collapse."

longevity: (lon-**jev**-i-tee) **noun** – having a long life; length of service

synonyms: durability, endurance, lastingness, seniority, tenure

*Latin's "longaevus" means "of great age; ancient." The **longevity** of the Bowhead Whale defies believability. It can live for more than 200 years.*

memory word: lawn-Chevy

picture: An old Chevy pickup rusts on the front lawn of a house down the street. The owner passed away years ago and his son moved into the house. He's lived there for several years now. The *lawn Chevy* has endured a *long life* just sitting there so long.

pedantic: (puh-**dan**-tik) **adjective** – too narrowly concerned with scholarly matters; ostentatious in one's learning especially in trivialities

synonyms: academic, bookish, pedagogic, punctilious, sententious

*The Simpsons' Comic Book Guy exemplifies a **pedantic** person.*

memory word: Pat-Ann-Tick

picture: *Pat* and *Ann Tick,* a *bookish* couple of ticks, sit at a table in a library speed-reading through stacks of books. When one Tick finishes a book, the other says, "Do you feel smarter? You look smarter." Their *only concern is trivial scholarly matters*.

transient: (tran-zee-uhnt) **adjective** – not lasting or enduring

synonyms: brief, momentary, passing, provisional, temporary

Latin's "transire" means "cross over, pass away." Florida's population would shrink if the hurricane season lasted a lot longer. Thankfully for Floridians, it is transient.

memory word: Train-See it?

picture: They built a high-speed train track about a half mile from your house. You can see it from your back porch. You invite company over and they hear a high-pitched horn off in the distance, and ask what it could be. You point to the *passing* locomotive and say, *"Train. See it?"*

resilient: (ri-zil-yuhnt) **adjective** – springing back; quick to recover

synonyms: flexible, hardy, irrepressible, rebounding, tough

*Latin's "resilientem" means "inclined to leap or spring back." I've never known anyone so **resilient**: injured so badly, yet so quickly recovered and healed.*

memory word: Brazilian

picture: A renowned *Brazilian* medicine man lives deep in the Brazilian rain forest. His potions and methods help sick and injured people *recover very quickly*. They call him the *Brazilian*.

benevolent: (buh-**nev**-uh-luhnt) **adjective** – characterized by or expressing goodwill or kindly feelings; desiring to help others

synonyms: compassionate, humanitarian, magnanimous

*Latin's "benevolentia" means "good feeling, good will, kindness." Mother Theresa comes to mind when I think of a **benevolent** soul.*

memory word: Ben-Elephant

picture: Ben the Elephant wanders around town with a smile on his face, ***helping people*** all day long. He tows cars that break down or run out of gas, helps fell trees, etc. ***Ben Elephant*** doesn't expect anything in return, he just likes ***expressing goodwill***.

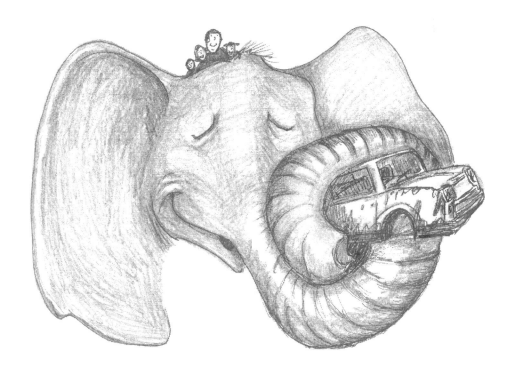

venerable: (ven-er-uh-buhl) **adjective** – commanding respect due to great age, dignity or accomplishment

synonyms: dignified, esteemed, honorable, imposing, revered

Latin's "venerari" means "to worship, revere." The **venerable** *old man garnered respect because of his contributions to the community.*

memory word: Winner-Bull

picture: The winningest boxing champ of the world is *honored* for his supreme accomplishment in boxing. He's a massive and *imposing* man they call the *Winner Bull*.

enhance: (en-**hans**) **verb** – to raise to a higher degree; to raise the value or price of

synonyms: aggrandize, amplify, augment, intensify, magnify

*Latin's "altare" means "to raise high." The new CEO of the company made all the right changes to **enhance** the reputation of the company.*

memory word: in-hands

picture: You wake up with the special power to ***augment or intensify*** anything you touch with your hands. Picture something you want to ***amplify***. If nothing comes to mind, imagine a thirty-inch flat screen TV on your bedroom wall. You take it ***in hands*** and ***magnify*** it to a one-hundred-inch screen.

tactful: (**takt**-ful) **adjective** – having tact, common sense, or poise

synonyms: considerate, courteous, diplomatic, judicious, polite

*Telling the truth is always the best policy, but sometimes it is hard to be **tactful** when doing so.*

memory word: tack-full

picture: A tack sits at the dinner table of a horrible cook. He finishes the disgusting turtle casserole on his plate and pats his belly **politely**, and compliments the host. "This is an interesting, one-of-a-kind meal I will remember forever. How did you know turtle is one of my favorites?" The **tack** is **full** and full of it, but the host doesn't have to know it. Upon leaving, the guest **courteously** accepts a container full of leftovers.

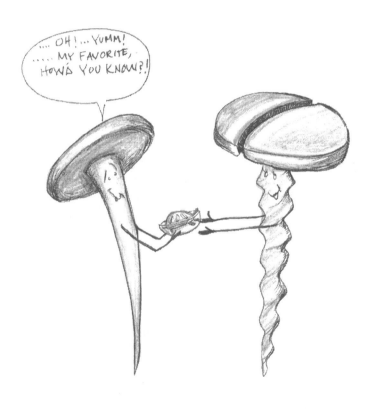

incompatible: (in-kuhm-**pat**-uh-buhl) **adjective** – unable to exist together in harmony; cannot coexist or be conjoined

synonyms: incongruous, mismatched, opposed, unsuitable

*My boss offered me a new position at work, but the hours were **incompatible** with my family life.*

memory word: in-come-Pat-and-Bill

picture: You and your friends sit at a coffee shop discussing the quarrelsome brothers, Pat and Bill. The siblings' rich father promised a million dollars to each son if they could learn to live in harmony in the same house for one full year. Speak of the devils, ***in come Pat and Bill.*** They are in each other's face, arguing over some disagreement as usual.

precocious: (pri-**koh**-shuhs) **adjective** – unusually advanced or mature in development, especially mental development

synonyms: advanced, bright, developed, mature

*Latin's "praecox" means "maturing early; ripened too soon." My daughter displayed a **precocious** ability in mathematics.*

memory word: green-coat-cash

picture: An eight-year-old boy wins the Masters Tournament. He is the youngest to ever win the ***green coat*** and ***cash*** prize. Talk about ***unusually advanced***! (The Masters is a professional golf tournament held each April. The first-prize winner receives a green jacket and almost one and a half million dollars, as of 2013. The total purse is eight million dollars.)

avert: (uh-**vurt**) **verb** – to turn away or aside; to ward off

synonyms: avoid, deflect, deter, divert, forestall, preclude, prevent

Latin's "avertere" means "to turn away." Far too many people resign themselves to an out-of-control federal government, and to politicians trampling on the Constitution. Not Mark Levin, the author of The Liberty Amendments: Restoring the American Republic. *Read it, and join the effort to restore the Constitution. It may be the only chance we have to* **avert** *disaster.*

memory word: a-vurp

picture: *A vurp* is when you burp and simultaneously vomit a little bit in the back of your mouth. Don't pretend you've never done it after a very large meal. Picture conjoined twins. One of them habitually vurps. When he does, his twin says, "C'mon dude. Can't you **turn away** when you vurp? That's disgusting."

suppress: (suh-**pres**) **verb** – to put an end to the activities of a person or thing; to keep in or repress; to withhold from disclosure or publication

synonyms: check, contain, curb, put down, quell, restrain, silence

*Latin's "supprimere" means "press down, stop, check, contain." I don't know why it works, but if I want to **suppress** a sneeze, I merely touch the side of my nose.*

memory word: soup-rest

picture: A miniature nurse stands on the back of your tongue, feeding chicken soup to your uvula. Your uvula and throat are sore from coughing. The nurse pats your uvula and says, "Shhhh. There, there, it's all right. All you need is **soup, rest,** and some TLC to **quell** your coughing.

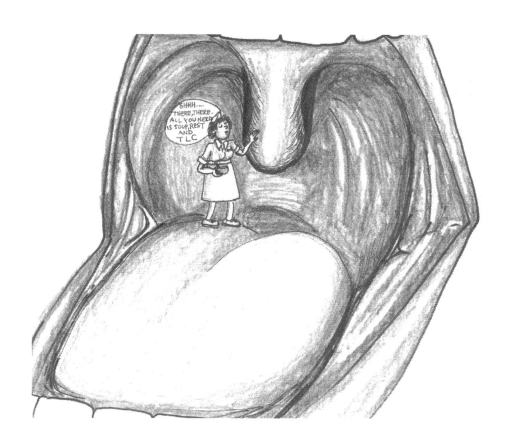

haughty: (haw-tee) **adjective** – disdainfully proud; scornfully arrogant

synonyms: contemptuous, overbearing, scornful, snobbish, uppity

*He should spend just one day as a waiter, then maybe he wouldn't act so **haughty** to the wait staff.*

memory word: hottie

picture: A supermodel signs her autograph for a teenage girl. The girl takes the opportunity to ask her for some tips on how she, too, can become a model. The supermodel looks her up and down ***disdainfully***. "You gotta be a ***hottie*** like me. My advice to you is to stay in school and study hard." She ***snobbishly turns her nose up*** and saunters away.

sagacious: (suh-**gay**-shuhs) **adjective** – having good judgment and understanding

synonyms: astute, insightful, perceptive, perspicacious, wise

Latin's "sagacis" means to "of quick perception." My grandpa has a reputation for being **sagacious**. *People often go to him for advice.*

memory word: the-day-shift

picture: You are hired to work at a vampire prison. Your boss asks, "Do you want **the day shift** or the…" You answer before he can finish the question, because you know the vampires will sleep during **the day shift**. You don't want to even think about the night shift. He responds, "I see you have **good judgment**."

evanescent: (ev-uh-**nes**-uhnt) **adjective** – vanishing; fading away

synonyms: fleeting, momentary, passing, temporary, tenuous, transient

*Latin's "evanescere" means "disappear, vanish." The memory of last night's dream is **evanescent**.*

memory word: Evan-a-scent

picture: Evan has a serious crush on a pretty girl in math class. She walks by and leaves *Evan a scent* of her perfume. He closes his eyes and inhales deeply through his nose, enjoying the moment, knowing the whiff of her is *fleeting*.

opulent: (**op**-yuh-luhnt) **adjective** – characterized by or exhibiting wealth, riches, or affluence; richly supplied

synonyms: extravagant, exuberant, lavish, luxurious, ostentatious

Latin's "opulentus" means "wealthy, rich." Some movie stars live an opulent lifestyle and some don't.

memory word: mop-you-lent

picture: Your wealthy neighbor's maid loans you a mop. It features an *ostentatious* gold handle, *lavishly* encrusted with expensive jewels. You return it, and say, "Here's the ***mop you lent*** to me."

camaraderie: (kah-muh-**rah**-duh-ree) **noun** – the feeling of friendship and trust among people who work or spend a lot of time together

synonyms: amity, comradeship, friendship, togetherness, unity

There's a special **camaraderie** *among military personnel and veterans.*

memory word: Camaro-Roddery

picture: Two buddies attend the annual *Camaro Roddery* hot rod car show. The guys share something in common...Camaros. They high-five and compliment each other's hotrods. Next year they'll do it all over again, and rekindle their *friendships and togetherness*.

inconsequential: (in-kon-si-**kwen**-shuhl) **adjective** – of little or no importance

synonyms: immaterial, insignificant, trifling, trivial, unimportant

*Latin's "inconsequentem" means "not logically connected." The engineer, focused on the overall design of the project, does not concern himself with **inconsequential** details.*

memory word: ink-on-sequined-shell

picture: A careless octopus accidentally spills some of his ink on a sea shell ornately decorated with sequins. He apologizes profusely for getting **ink on sequined shell**, but the shell says, "Don't give it another thought. Really it's **no big deal, insignificant** at best, the least of my worries."

nonchalant: (non-shuh-**lahnt**) **adjective** – marked by blithe unconcern or indifference

synonyms: blasé, casual, cool, disinterested, dispassionate

Even though he had a massive crush on her, he played it cool and just gave her a **nonchalant** *smile when she walked by.*

memory word: None-Shall-Want

picture: As a billionaire, you created the ***None Shall Want*** Foundation through which you donate millions of dollars to needy families. After giving a million dollars to a destitute family, a reporter asks you how it feels to help this family. Always ***easygoing and casual,*** you say, "It's no big deal, I do it every day."

divergent: (dih-**vur**-juhnt) **adjective** – tending to move apart in different directions; diverging from each other or a standard

synonyms: deviating, disagreeing, disparate, separate, unalike

*Latin's "divergere" means "to go in different directions." We went through twelve years of school and four years of college together, but from there we took **divergent** paths.*

memory word: diver-gents

picture: Two scuba diver gentlemen exit a boat to begin their underwater exploring excursion. The ***diver gents move apart*** and swim in ***different directions***.

reclusive: (rek-loos-iv) **adjective** – withdrawn from society; seeking solitude

synonyms: cloistered, isolated, monastic, secluded, sequestered

*Do you remember Howard Hughes, the famous **reclusive** millionaire?*

memory word: Ray-clue-live

picture: You go on a camping trip with a group, but *withdraw from the group* to set up your own little campsite in a nearby cave. The entrance collapses, leaving you trapped. A ray of light shines through a hole in the cave's ceiling. This *ray* is the *clue* to how you will save yourself to *live* another day. If you can make it to the hole, you can widen the hole and escape.

jaunty: (**jawn**-tee) **adjective** – having a cheerful, lively, and self-confident manner

synonyms: chipper, high spirited, perky, sprightly, vivacious

*She whistled as she walked down the street with a **jaunty** step.*

memory word: John-T.

picture: There goes *John T.* He's always *cheerful* and walks with a *spring in his step* as if he just won the lottery.

esoteric: (es-uh-**ter**-ik) **adjective** – understood by or meant for only the select few who have special knowledge or interest

synonyms: abstruse, arcane, inscrutable, obscure, orphic, recondite

Greek's "esoterikos" means "belonging to an inner circle." The Freemasons, an **esoteric** *fraternal organization, originated in the late 16th century.*

memory word: that's-so-Derek

picture: There's a boy in your school named Derek and you see him talking to a stranger. The stranger hands him a sealed envelope labeled *"Top Secret"* and walks away. When Derek walks by, you ask, "Who's the mysterious dude and what's in the envelope?" He responds, "If I told you, I'd have to kill you!" *That's so Derek.*

censure: (**sen**-sher) **noun/verb** – a strong expression of disapproval; an official reprimand by a legislative body of one of its members; to criticize or reproach in a harsh manner

synonyms: admonishment, condemnation, rebuke, reproof

Latin's "censura" means "judgment, opinion." When a member of Congress is **censured***, he is not removed from his elected office. However, the member does lose any committee chairs he holds.*

memory word: Sin?-Sure!

picture: The Pope asks you if you sinned and you reply, *"Sin? Sure!"* He whacks you on top of your head with his mitre (ceremonial hat) giving you a good *reprimand*.

desultory: (**des**-uhl-tawr-ee) **adjective** – marked by a lack of a definite plan or purpose; jumping from one thing to another

synonyms: aimless, deviating, erratic, haphazard, rambling

The word desultory is derived from Latin's "desultor." A desultor was a skilled circus rider who jumped from the back of one galloping horse or chariot to another. High-school reunions often involve many **desultory** *conversations.*

memory word: the-salt-tree

picture: As a contestant on a game show, you have a chance to win one thousand dollars if you can pick all the salt shakers off of *the salt tree* in thirty seconds. You pick a shaker, then *jump to the other side* of the tree and continue this nonsense until you hear the buzzer. You *didn't have an organized plan* or strategy so you didn't pick all of the salt shakers and win the money.

capricious: (kuh-**pree**-shuhs) **adjective** – showing sudden changes in attitude or behavior; lacking firmness or steadiness

synonyms: erratic, fickle, impulsive, inconsistent, unpredictable

*With my **capricious** boss, I never know if Jekyll or Hyde will show up for work.*

memory word: the-breezes

picture: You're in a beautiful Hawaiian Lagoon on a sail board trying to learn how to wind surf. However, every time you pick up some momentum, the breeze *changes directions* and you come to a stop, lose balance, and fall off. *The breezes, erratic and inconsistent,* leave you frustrated.

incorrigible: (in-**kawr**-i-juh-buhl) **adjective** – impossible to correct, control, or change

synonyms: intractable, unmanageable, unreformable

Latin's "incorrigibilis" means "not to be corrected." Her boyfriend, an **incorrigible** *flirt, flashed a megawatt smile at her.*

memory word: encourage-a-bull

picture: A father bull plays bullfighter with his son. He waves a red flag, enticing his son to charge at it. He tells him, "You'll make a great bullfighter killer someday." Mom says, "Don't encourage him. You know once he starts down that road it will be *impossible to change him*. You can *encourage a bull*, any bull, to do that, but not our little go-getter."

loathe: (lohth) **verb** – to feel disgust or intense aversion for

synonyms: abhor, despise, detest, hate, revolt

*I like almost every genre of music, but I must admit I **loathe** disco.*

memory word: load

picture: Imagine a mother with fifteen kids along with the sheer volume of laundry she must do every day. Her husband comes home from work, asks her about her day, and she explodes, "Do you have any idea how much I ***detest*** doing laundry? One more ***load*** and I will snap!"

hiatus: (high-**ay**-tuhs) **noun** – a break or interruption in continuity; a gap or opening

synonyms: interim, interval, pause, reprieve, respite, suspension

Hiatus is a loanword from Latin. *My favorite rock band's tour is on* **hiatus** *until the singer's strained vocal cords heal.*

memory word: hate-us

picture: The elves, merrily working in Santa's Workshop, spontaneously break out into "Jingle Bells" and *the work stops*. Santa hits an elf on the top of the head and tells him to get back to work. After Santa leaves, the elf whimpers, "Why does he *hate us*?"

condescending: (kon-duh-**sen**-ding) **adjective** – behaving as though you are more important and intelligent than other people

synonyms: arrogant, disdainful, patronizing, snobbish, superior

Latin's "condescendere" means "to let oneself down." He responded to the reporter's probing questions with only **condescending** *and flippant comments.*

memory word: candy-sending

picture: An *arrogant* little girl goes to school the day after Halloween with a big bag of candy. She says, "I was so incredibly popular and successful Trick-Or-Treating. Everyone loved my homemade costume so much they rewarded me with extra candy. I'm shipping most of it to homeless shelters throughout the state, so I'll be doing a lot of *candy sending*, but I had so much more than all of you, I thought I could spare some to share."

abnegate: (ab-ni-gayt) **verb** – to refuse or deny oneself an indulgence; relinquish power or responsibility

synonyms: abstain, decline, give up, refrain, reject, renounce

*Latin's "abnegare" means "to refuse, deny." As the CEO neared retirement, she began to **abnegate** some of her responsibilities to her likely successor.*

memory word: have-no-cake

picture: When Jeffy tipped the scales at four-hundred pounds, he said, "Enough is enough! From this day forward, I will ***have no cake**. I **renounce** cake and all other sweets."

hypothesis: (hahy-**poth**-uh-sis) **noun** – an idea or explanation of something based on a few known facts but has not yet been proved to be true or correct

synonyms: conjecture, proposition, speculation, supposition

*This is a loanword from Greek to Latin to English. My massage therapist is "out there." She has a **hypothesis** that when we dream we literally move into an alternate universe.*

memory word: fly-pod-thesis

picture: In the 1986 movie *The Fly*, a brilliant scientist transports himself -- and, unwittingly, a fly -- from one telepod to another. Over the next few weeks, he begins to turn into a half man, half fly creature. When he notices these changes, he comes up with his ***fly pod thesis*** as a *speculative explanation* for what is happening to him.

parched: (pahrcht) **adjective** – dried out by heat or excessive exposure to sunlight

synonyms: dehydrated, evaporated, scorched, thirsty, withered

Latin's "persiccare" means "to dry thoroughly." I returned from vacation to find my sprinkler system broken and my grass lawn **parched**.

memory word: marched

picture: A detachment of soldiers separated from the main body in a desert sand storm. They *marched* through the desert searching for the others until they *dried out*.

adulation: (aj-uh-**lay**-shuhn) **noun** – excessive devotion to someone; servile flattery

synonyms: bootlicking, fawning, flattery, sycophancy, worship

*My garage band enjoys the **adulation** of our small group of fans.*

memory word: flatulation

picture: One of the students in your class has a problem with *flatulation* (excessive gas). Something has to be done, so everyone chips in and buys him a boat load of Gas-B-Gone Ultra-Strength pills. The pills work and everyone goes overboard *fawning* over him, *flattering* him for his big accomplishment. Anything to keep him on the pills, right?

prosaic: (proh-**zay**-ik) **adjective** – commonplace or dull; having the character or form of prose rather than poetry

synonyms: everyday, hackneyed, humdrum, mundane, ordinary

*Latin's "prosus" means "straightforward, direct." Some live an exciting life on the edge, but most live on the more **prosaic** side of life.*

memory word: pros-say-it

picture: I hate the on-field or locker room interviews with the pro athletes after a game when they utter the ***common, hackneyed*** nonsense such as, "We have a good ball club and we gave it one hundred and ten percent out there today." When the ***pros say it***, I just roll my eyes.

inevitable: (in-**ev**-i-tuh-buhl) **adjective** – unable to be avoided, evaded, or escaped; sure to occur or happen

synonyms: assured, certain, destined, impending, unalterable

*Latin's "inevitabilis" means "unavoidable." Death is **inevitable**, no one can escape it.*

memory word: him-have-it-all

picture: In an old western movie you're watching with your family, a scene shows a couple of men seated at a table in a saloon, playing poker. You say, "I've never seen this movie, but I can tell you what is **sure to happen next**. One of the cowboys will accuse the other of cheating, and he'll draw his gun. Before he can shoot, the accused will let **him have it all** from his gun hidden under the table."

jubilant: (joo-buh-luhnt) **adjective** – filled with joy; extreme happiness

synonyms: elated, euphoric, exuberant, exultant, rhapsodic, thrilled

*Latin's 'jubilum' means "wild cry." The fans, **jubilant** when their team won the Superbowl, jumped up and down, screaming and yelling.*

memory word: jewel-ant

picture: The queen ant awards an ant with a pile of jewels. You can imagine how ***filled with joy*** the ***jewel ant*** feels as he dives into his newfound wealth.

superfluous: (soo-**pur**-floo-uhs) **adjective** – being more than is sufficient or required

synonyms: excessive, extravagant, lavish, nonessential, unnecessary

*Latin's "superfluere" means "to overflow." Not enough girls attended the dance, so the **superfluous** number of boys danced in groups.*

memory word: super-floss

picture: You buy huge spools of mega ***super floss*** at Sam's Club because you use a lot of it to floss your teeth. You don't just wrap some around your fingers, but all around both hands. No wonder your teeth gleem so clean and shiny.

hedonist: (**heed**-n-ist) **noun** – a person whose life is devoted to the pursuit of pleasure and self-gratification

synonyms: epicurean, glutton, profligate, sensualist, sybarite

*Greek's "hedone" means "pleasure." My congressman claims to act as a servant of the people, but in reality his only concern is to attend extravagant **hedonist** V.I.P parties.*

memory word: he-done-list

picture: A doctor tells his patient he has a rare terminal disease and only six months to live. The patient makes a bucket list full of **pleasure seeking**. He determines to finish the list before he kicks the bucket. At the end of six months *he done list* and feels very *self-gratified*.

anonymous: (uh-**non**-uh-muhs) **adjective** – a name not known or not made public

synonyms: nameless, uncredited, undisclosed, unidentified

Latin's "anonymus" means "without a name." A wealthy businessman donated a lot of money to the charter school my children attend. I want to personally thank him, but he wishes to remain **anonymous**.

memory word: a-non-name-mouse

picture: A mouse stands up on stage at a comedy club. He asks, "What do you call a mouse with *no name*?"

"That's right…**a non-name mouse**. Ba dum tshh."

compassion: (kuhm-**pash**-uhn) **noun** – a feeling of deep sympathy and sorrow for another who is stricken by misfortune, accompanied by a strong desire to alleviate the suffering

synonyms: benevolence, commiseration, empathy, tenderness

Latin's "compassionem" means "sympathy." Although stern and demanding, President George Washington also exhibited a lot of compassion.

memory word: compass-show

picture: Captain Ahab and his whaling ship crew scramble to gather all of their provisions and launch the life boats after Moby Dick rammed their ship. Shipwrecked a thousand miles away from land, Captain Ahab wants to get his bearings. He asks Starbuck, "What does the *compass show*?" How can you not have *sympathy* for their misfortune? (FYI: The name of the coffee chain Starbucks was inspired by the name of a character in the novel *Moby Dick*.)

maladroit: (mal-uh-**droit**) **adjective** – done without skill, especially in a way that annoys or offends people

synonyms: awkward, blundering, bumbling, clumsy, inept

*The Three Stooges are a bunch of bumbling, blundering, **maladroit** fools.*

memory word: mallet-droid

picture: In the future, Santa replaces his elves with droids. One of the droids on the assembly line, a ***mallet droid***, wields a rubber mallet to stamp everything rolling past. But, he needs recalibration. ***Clumsy and inept***, he misses half of the toys and crushes the ones he does stamp.

baleful: (**bayl**-fuhl) **adjective** – threatening or foreshadowing evil or tragic developments

synonyms: foreboding, harmful, malevolent, ominous, pernicious

*The weather report focused on the **baleful** hurricane threatening to barrel up the entire east coast.*

memory word: bale-fall

picture: You stand there minding your own business when someone shouts, "Hay!" and points up above you. You look up to see an ***ominous*** bale of hay falling directly overhead. This ***bale fall*** will not be pretty.

adversity: (ad-**vur**-si-tee) **noun** – a difficult or unpleasant situation

synonyms: distress, hardship, hard times, misfortune, suffering, trial

*Latin's "adversitas" means "opposition." President Abraham Lincoln faced many personal and public **adversities**.*

memory word: Ad-Versity

picture: The Advertising University will soon open its doors to students who want to learn everything about advertising. The day before classes start, an earthquake levels the whole **Ad-Versity** campus complex. Talk about **misfortune and distress**.

feign: (fayn) **verb** – to represent fictitiously; put on an appearance with the intent to deceive

synonyms: affect, bluff, fake, invent, pretend, put on act

*Latin's "fingere" means "to touch, handle; devise, contrive." When she called in sick, her boss couldn't discern if she only **feigned** a cough or if it was the real thing.*

memory word: fang

picture: You and your friends indulge in a *Twilight* DVD movie marathon over the weekend. You show up at school Monday morning wearing some plastic vampire *fangs* and funky contact lenses *pretend*ing to be a vampire.

impetuous: (im-**pech**-oo-uhs) **adjective** – acting or done quickly and without thinking carefully about the results

synonyms: impulsive, precipitate, rash, spontaneous, unplanned

*Latin's "impetus" means "attack, charge." Brash and **impetuous** in his youth, these days he acts reserved and calculated.*

memory word: um-pet-your-asp

picture: Your family vacations in India. You stroll along in the market area and see a snake charmer displaying his skills with a highly poisonous asp (another name for a cobra). You reach out to touch the asp and he shrieks, "No, no, no! What are you doing?" You respond, "I, **um, pet your asp**."

anachronism: (uh-**nak**-ruh-niz-uhm) **noun** – something or someone not in the correct historical or chronological time, especially a thing or person belonging to an earlier time

synonyms: incongruity, misdate, misplacement, prochronism

*Latin's "anachronismus" means "refer to wrong time." An **anachronism** occurs in a scene in The Alamo with John Wayne: a yellow school bus drives along a dusty road in the background.*

memory word: an-afro-prism

picture: Your favorite basketball star wears a big geometrically shaped afro. When the sunlight hits it just right, it creates a rainbow prism effect. He teleports to **an earlier time** in the Roman Forum, and asks senators if they want to play some basketball. Julius Caesar walks up and asks him, "What is that on your head?" He says, "it's **an afro prism,** bro."

mete: (meet) **verb** – to distribute or apportion by measure (usually followed by out)

synonyms: allocate, apportion, dispense, dole, measure, ration

Latin's "meta" means "goal, end, boundary, pillar." "For with what judgment ye judge, ye shall be judged: and with what measure ye **mete***, it shall be measured to you again." (Matthew 7:2)*

memory word: meat

picture: Some kids come home from school one day indoctrinated by their teacher to convert to a vegetarian diet. They say the teacher told them *"meat* is murder." The mom's turn to provide a nutritious snack for the kids happens to fall on the next day. She delivers equally *measured portions* of *meat* pie, much to the teacher's dismay.

boorish: (**boor**-ish) **adjective** – ill mannered, coarse, and contemptible in behavior or appearance

synonyms: barbaric, loutish, oafish, rude, uncouth, vulgar

*Our **boorish** dinner guest chewed with his mouth open, and told off-color jokes.*

memory word: boar-shhhhh!

picture: A boar visits a setting where people are expected to remain quiet and well mannered, such as a library, church, or wedding ceremony. The boar ruins it for everyone. He burps loudly, makes fart noises with his armpit, and acts generally ***rude and vulgar***. People say, ***"Boar! Shhhhh!"***

procrastinate: (proh-**kras**-tuh-nayt) **verb** – to delay doing something that should be done

synonyms: dawdle, defer, hesitate, postpone

*Latin's "procrastinare" means "to put off till tomorrow; postpone, delay." Most students hate to do term papers, thus they **procrastinate** until the last minute.*

memory word: Grow-Grass-In-Eight

picture: The front lawn of a guy on the block turns brown. One of his neighbors asks when he's going to over-seed with winter grass. He says, "Yeah, I got some of that there Miracle ***Grow Grass In Eight*** Days winter rye, but I keep saying I'll get to it next weekend."

beleaguer: (bih-**lee**-ger) **verb** – to annoy persistently; to surround with military forces

synonyms: badger, beset, bother, harass, nag, pester, siege, vex

*The whole teaching staff **beleaguers** the new school principal with complaints and concerns.*

memory word: B-leager

picture: A scrawny kid on the playground wants to play basketball with the other kids. They **surround** him and **badger** him. "You're a **B-leager**. You can't run, dribble, pass, jump, or shoot. Go home and play dolls with your sister."

intuitive: (in-**too**-i-tiv) **adjective** – obtained by using your feelings rather than by considering the facts

synonyms: instinctual, perceptive, untaught, visceral

Latin's "intueri" means "look at; consider, regard." Her **intuitive** *senses screamed at her, "Don't believe a word he says! He's lying!"*

memory word: into-a-tiff

picture: Picture a very intuitive person. He regrets a bad decision and flies **into a tiff** because he didn't listen to his **instincts**. He purchased a stock based on what the experts said, and lost money. He throws his hands up in the air exclaiming, "That does it! From now on, if it doesn't **feel** right, I don't buy it."

ostentatious: (os-ten-**tay**-shuhs) **adjective** – characterized by pretentious or conspicuous show in an attempt to impress others

synonyms: exhibitionistic, flamboyant, flaunted, garish

My neighbor displays his newfound wealth in an **ostentatious** *manner every day, with new cars, a speed boat, flashy jewelry, etc.*

memory word: Austin-Texas

picture: A lot of rich people in *Austin Texas* attend the annual Peacock Festival. They spend a lot of money raising and showing off their prize peacocks in an effort to *display their wealth*.

novice: (**nov**-is) **noun** – a person who is new and has little experience in a skill or activity

synonyms: amateur, beginner, greenhorn, neophyte, rookie

*Latin's "novicius" means "new, fresh, inexperienced" (usually refers to someone recently enslaved). Auto insurance is much more expensive for **novice** drivers.*

memory word: know-this

picture: You take Drivers Ed, which makes you an *amateur* driver. Your Drivers Ed instructor acts a little odd. He sticks his index finger up in the air and says *"know this"* when he wants to make an important point for you to remember. The very first day of class he says, "OK, *neophytes, know this!"*

lobbyist: (lob-ee-ist) **noun** – a person who tries to influence legislation on behalf of a special interest

synonyms: activist, influence peddler, powerbroker

Many retiring senators and congressmen transition smoothly into lucrative careers as ***lobbyists***.

memory word: law-beast

picture: Lobbyists represent special interest groups including Planned Parenthood, AFL/CIO, National Farmers Union, Americans For Tax Reform, Gun Owners of America, etc. They meet with lawmakers schmoozing them with expensive gifts, vacations, cash, etc. They purposefully **influence** the legislator to pass laws favoring their interests over others. Picture a lobbyist to rival all others -- a *law beast*. He doesn't need to buy politicians off with goodies. He scares them into writing and passing laws to benefit his interests.

pretentious: (pri-**ten**-shuhs) **adjective** – trying to appear important, intelligent, etc., to impress other people

synonyms: affected, bombastic, put-on, showy, vainglorious

Latin's "praetendere" means "to stretch in front, put forward." Despite her immense wealth, extreme beauty, and superb education, she did not display the slightest **pretentiousness***.*

memory word: pretend-shoes

picture: A little girl rummages through her parents' closet playing dress up. She slips on a pair of mom's shoes, puts on a **pompous** air, and says, "OK, these are my *pretend shoes*. When I put them on, I'm a walking, talking Wikipedia. Ask me anything and I'll tell you all about it. Impressive huh?"

conditional: (kuhn-**dish**-uh-nl) **adjective** – imposing, containing, subject to, or depending on a condition or conditions

synonyms: contingent, provisional, qualified, subject to, tentative

Latin's "condicere" means "to speak with, talk together." To maintain her **conditional** *scholarship, an Ivy League school required the Valedictorian to maintain a mere 4.0 GPA until graduation.*

memory word: Kahn-dish-and-all

picture: Genghis Kahn and his band of warriors invade your home and threaten to kill your whole family. Well, he picked the wrong house. Your whole family is a bunch of heat pack'n, Second Amendment-cherishing, Ted Nugent loving, National Rifle Association members. The tables turn when your family draws their guns on Kahn and the boys. Your pistol pack'n mama arranges a *conditional* surrender for them. She says they can walk away on their own two feet instead of being carried away in body bags, but only after **Kahn** does the **dishes and all** of the family's chores. Didn't Kahn's dad teach him never to bring a sword to a gunfight?

orator: (or-uh-ter) **noun** – one who is good at making formal speeches

synonyms: lecturer, pontificator, public speaker, rhetorician

*Orator is a loanword from Latin. Cicero, the renowned Roman **orator**, is considered history's finest speaker.*

memory word: oar-at-oar

picture: Two oars go at it in a public speaking debate to determine the best orator. It reaches a heated pitch when both oars leave their podiums and come face-to-face in a back-and-forth, ***oar-at-oar*** banter.

amicable: (am-i-kuh-buhl) **adjective** – characterized by goodwill

synonyms: agreeable, amiable, friendly, neighborly, peaceful

*Latin's "amicus" means "friend." The two parties successfully reached an **amicable** settlement without requiring a trial.*

memory word: hammock-able

picture: Hammocks hold almost magical powers. Spend an hour in one and you will be a much more **agreeable** person. Grumpy people need only a hammock. They are **hammockable**.

inveigle: (in-**vay**-guhl) **verb** – to achieve control over somebody in a clever and dishonest way, especially so they will do what you want

synonyms: cajole, charm, coax, con, influence, persuade, snow

*Of course I didn't recognize him as a con-man when he **inveigled** me into investing in his pyramid scheme.*

memory word: Ian-bagel

picture: Your friend Ian loves bagels. You tempt him to help you cheat on a test. His mom is the math teacher, so he can acquire the test questions ahead of time. You promise to supply him with bagels the remainder of the school year if he will help you cheat on the next math test. The next test day you hold a bag of bagels out and say, "**Ian, bagels.**"

restrained: (ri-**straynd**) **adjective** – showing calm control rather than emotion

synonyms: controlled, cool, in check, temperate, under wraps

*Latin's "restringere" means "fasten behind one, tie up." The riot police **restrained** themselves admirably in the face of the lawless protesters.*

memory word: rest-trained

picture: You stress out easily. You become anxious, suffer migraine headaches, endure sweaty palms, and see spots when under stress. You visit a therapist for tips on how to reduce your tensions. She hooks you up to a machine displaying your stress level and heart rate on a screen. She trains you to rest your mind, body, and soul in the face of anxiety. You might say she ***rest trained*** you. The new and improved ***rest trained*** you, shows uncommon ***calm, control, and inhibition*** in all situations.

gloat: (gloht) **verb** – to show you are happy about your own success or somebody else's failure, in an unpleasant way

synonyms: exult, relish, rub it in, vaunt, whoop

*The James Madison Prep Patriots shut out their opponent, but characteristically did not **gloat**.*

memory word: goat

picture: Two mountain goats go at it, butting horns. The winner is not a good winner. He displays his prowess, ***rubs it in***, and flexes his muscles while the defeated ***goat*** licks his wounds.

prosperity: (pro-**sper**-i-tee) **noun** – a successful, flourishing, or thriving condition, especially in the financial realm

synonyms: abundance, boom, fortune, good times, increase, plenty

Latin's "prosperare" means "cause to succeed, render happy." Growth and **prosperity** *characterize the decades following WWII.*

memory word: wasp-parrot-tee

picture: A wealthy wasp and parrot meet every morning for an eight o'clock tee time, which means the **wasp parrot tee** off for golf at that time. So **rich and successful**, they no longer having to work, they engage in many leisure activities such as golf.

revere: (ri-**veer**) **verb** – to feel great respect or admiration for somebody or something

synonyms: adore, cherish, esteem, exalt, honor, venerate, worship

Latin's "revereri" means "to stand in awe of, respect, honor, fear." His loyal troops **revere** *the highly decorated general.*

memory word: Paul-Revere

picture: The residents of Revere, Massachusetts, greatly **respect and admire Paul Revere**. Their **esteem** prompted them to name their town after him.

inure: (in-**noor**) **verb** – to cause to accept or become hardened to difficulty, pain, or something unpleasant

synonyms: acclimate, familiarize, habituate, season, toughen, train

*The prisoners quickly **inure** themselves to the harsh conditions in Sheriff Joe's Tent City jail.*

memory word: in-your

picture: A teenage boy's bedroom smells like a foul, stinky garbage pit. He's **acclimated to** the filth and stench, but not his parents. They don't dare enter. Mom knocks on the door, and he invites her in. She says, "No way am I coming **in your** room. I just wanted you to know dinner is ready."

aesthetic: (es-**thet**-ik) **adjective** – concerning or characterized by an appreciation of beauty or good taste

synonyms: artful, artistic, beautiful, creative, gorgeous

*The extremely rustic furniture in my house is more **aesthetic** than functional.*

memory word: athletic

picture: An athlete, whose body is the epitome of athleticism and **beauty**, handstands on the balance beam. She maintains a pose while holding a mirror with her feet to apply lipstick. She displays her *athletic* and *artistic* qualities.

About The Author

Shayne Gardner is a former history teacher who constantly encouraged his students to develop a strong vocabulary. He put a new word on the whiteboard every day and quizzed the students every Friday. The students who turned the words into pictures, as instructed, aced the quizzes every week.

Shayne lives with his wife and daughter in Chandler, Arizona. He would prefer to reside in Hawaii, so please purchase several copies of this book and gift them to family and friends.

VisualizeYourVocabulary@gmail.com

VisualizeYourVocabulary.com

Facebook.com/VisualizeYourVocabulary

Index

Made in the USA
Lexington, KY
16 October 2015